Creating Sustainable Environments in our Schools

edited by Tony Shallcross, John Robinson,
Paul Pace and Arjen Wals

Trentham Books

Stoke on Trent, UK and Sterling, USA

Trentham Books Limited
Westview House   22883 Quicksilver Drive
734 London Road   Sterling
Oakhill   VA 20166-2012
Stoke on Trent   USA
Staffordshire
England ST4 5NP

First published 2006

British Library Cataloguing-in-Publication Data
A catalogue record for this book is available from the British Library

ISBN-13: 978-1-85856-352-7
ISBN-10: 1-85856-352-6

Designed and typeset by Trentham Print Design Ltd, Chester and printed in Great Britain by Cromwell Press Ltd, Trowbridge.

Contents

List of figures, Tables and Appendices
Figures

Tables

Foreword

Our biggest challenge in this new century is to take an idea that sounds abstract – sustainable development – and turn it into reality for all the world's people (Kofi Annan, United Nations Secretary General).

This book aims to encourage and assist schools, headteachers, teachers, administrative staff, pupils and communities to develop whole school approaches as one way of turning sustainable development into reality. It examines some current European thinking about school development, whole school approaches, self-evaluation and the professional development of teachers. Case studies from the field of environmental education (EE) and education for sustainable development (ESD) illustrate how whole school approaches might develop. The case studies are drawn from England, Finland, Greece, Malta and Portugal. The final chapter explores sources of support for schools seeking to develop whole school approaches.

The notion of whole school development is explored in the context of EE and ESD, primarily because both are consistently committed to changing values, attitudes and actions so that these become more consistent with and supportive of sustainable living. Examples of values, attitudes and actions that reflect social and environmental justice feature throughout the book and especially in the case studies in Chapters Six to Ten and in Chapters Two and Three. Schools have an important role to play in promoting and practising sustainable living by making links between sustainable development, professional development and school development. These links are explored in this book. Linking EE and ESD with major educational movements such as school development should make EE and ESD more prominent in mainstream education.

The view taken in this book is that whole school approaches represent one, and possibly the most successful, educational strategy, for closing gaps but also for forging links between knowledge, attitudes and sustainable actions. A second reason is that the contributors to this book were involved in a European Commission funded project: Sustainability Education in European Primary Schools (SEEPS) (Shallcross, 2004). Finally, 2005 marked the start of UNESCO Decade of ESD (UN DESD, 2005-2014) (see Chapter Eleven). We hope that his book will make a timely contribution to the realisation of the aims of this decade.

SECTION A

Clarifying terms

Introduction
Mind your Es, Ds and Ss: clarifying some terms

Tony Shallcross and Arjen E.J. Wals

A: Environmental education (EE) and education for sustainable development (ESD)

Arguments about terminology abound in the EE/ESD literature. We do not intend to indulge in definition dementia or lengthy debate about which of the many terms that are used to describe approaches to education that address the environment and/or sustainability are correct. But readers need some understanding of terms such as EE (UNESCO 1978), earth education (van Matre, 1990), education for sustainability (EfS) (Huckle and Sterling, 1996), sustainable education (Sterling, 2001), sustainability education (SE) (Shallcross, 2004), education as sustainability (EaS) (Foster, 2001), education for a sustainable future (ESF) (UNESCO, 1997) ESD (UNESCO, 2004) and learning for sustainability (LfS) (WWF, 2005) and others.

As the case studies illustrate, different terms are used in different contexts and countries to describe the concepts and approaches to whole school development and whole school approaches advocated in this text. Debates about semantics do not readily engage school staff, especially those working in primary schools, because their main preoccupation is to deal with the practical daily realities of schooling children (Alexander, 1984). Some authors (Wilson, 2002) argue that it is more important for EE/ESD to focus on action and agreement than on adversarial academic exchanges that terminate at debate and dispute. We are not arguing for imposed consensus or the suppression of critical thinking that may at times involve dissonance and conflict. Our plea is for an approach through which the people engaged in debates about EE/ESD can focus on critical searches for agreement that

3

lead to action now or sow the seeds of future action. This argument is developed further in Chapters Two and Four.

As the terms EE/ESD are used throughout this book some exploration of the debates behind the use of these terms might be helpful. The term ESD has to some extent superseded EE in Europe and perhaps the world in recent years. The advent of the United Nations Decade of Education for Sustainable Development 2005-2014 (UN DESD) has been significant in generating this change in terminology. Terminology has evolved away from the term EE, partly because of a number of problems associated with its use.

Although it is often argued that EE is education about, for, in and through the environment, this has not prevented some educationalists from using the term in narrower senses and particularly to mean education about the environment. Environmental studies is a better term to describe education with this solely cognitive focus. But some who use EE in this narrow cognitive sense advocate environmental studies in the mistaken belief that if people become aware of environmental issues they will act for their resolution (Sterling, 2001) (see Chapter Two).

Another problem that has bedevilled EE is that it is sometimes associated solely with the green or natural environment and not with the social, economic or built environments. This is the view taken in the Draft UN DESD Strategy (2004), which states that EE '...is a well-established discipline that focuses on humankind's relationship with the natural environment and on ways to conserve and preserve it and properly steward its resources' (UNESCO, 2004: 21). However in some European countries such as Scotland, EE based on the influential writings of Sir Patrick Geddes has consistently been associated with education that is about, for in and through the natural, social and economic environments, a view that UNESCO subscribed to in its 1978 description of EE:

> To foster clear awareness of, and concern about, economic, social, political and ecological interdependence in urban and rural areas; to provide every person with opportunities to acquire the knowledge, values, attitudes commitment and skills needed to protect and improve the environment; to create new patterns of behaviour of individuals, groups and society as a whole towards the environment. (UNESCO, 1978)

What this debate shows is that a universal definition of a term such as EE is impossible and so any debate purely about semantics is largely irrelevant. Those who advocate EE/ESD should not only be seeking to clarify terms such as EE and ESD in the local contexts to which these terms are applied, such as schools (Stables, 2001) but also to use EE/ESD to develop these contexts in a sustainable manner. This process is dynamic because it will lead to evolving descriptions and definitions of terms such as EE/ESD, rather than quests for incontestable meaning. This definitional dilemma is illustrated by Tooley's (2000) assertion that sustainable development, a concept supported by all European Union (EU) governments, is part of an anti-capitalist agenda. However this debate about terminology is important when it exposes the paucity of educational definitions that describe outcomes based approaches to EE/ESD.

A change in terminology towards the notion of educations linked with sustainability or sustainable development might well be useful. This change has been influenced by international events, most notably the World Commission on Environment and Development's report (WCED) *Our Common Future* (1987) and the 1992 Earth Summit (Quarrie, 1992) (see Chapter Eleven). *Our Common Future* produced one of the most widely used definitions of sustainable development '...improving the quality of human life while living within the carrying capacity of supporting ecosystems' (43). These disparate developments spawned a number of the educational terms that linked education with sustainability or sustainable development, such as ESD, EfS and ESF but in so doing some of these terms have raised other controversies.

Objections were raised to the terms EfS (Jickling, 1992) and ESD. These objections focused on the word 'for'. How could we have education for sustainability or sustainable development when we only have the vaguest understandings of what these terms mean or what sustainable societies will look like? This argument is developed further in Chapters Three and Four. Others object to the term sustainable development (Shiva, 1992, Sachs, 1995) because it equates sustainability with economic sustainability, the quantitative notion of maintaining yields and consumption levels, for example, from sustainable forests. Shiva and Sachs argue for ecological sustainability, the qualitative regard for the richness and variety of flora and fauna involved in sustaining biodiversity. Ecological sustainability requires humanity to try to improve and at worst not reduce biodiveristy in its quest for economically sustainable production.

Our analysis should go beyond definitions and examine the concepts and practices that inform such definitions as we have illustrated here with EE/ESD. But if the 1997 UNESCO description of ESD is compared to the 1978 UNESCO description of EE some strong similarities emerge:

...the effectiveness of awareness raising and education for sustainable development must ultimately be measured by the extent to which they change the attitudes and behaviours of people as both consumers and citizens. Changes in lifestyles as reflected in individual behaviour, households and at a community level must take place. (UNESCO, 1997: 4)

Although the description had changed by 1997, the commitment to changing knowledge, attitudes and actions so that these support sustainable lifestyles can be traced from the discussions of EE in 1978 to deliberations over ESD in 1997 and in the UNESCO Draft Strategy on the DESD (2004). If schools are to become places that deliberate, promote and enact sustainable actions there has to be a stronger focus on whole school development to model sustainable living in EE/ESD with self-evaluation as a key process. Whole school approaches emphasise processes rather than the outcomes of education. It is crucial that values, attitudes and actions change in ways that equip pupils with the personal, social and environmental competences to live in harmony with the world around them. Change of this magnitude in education entails the professional development of school staff. But the focus on process in EE/ESD is not a panacea, because processes can be hierarchical or participatory and linked to a passive or empowered citizenry as shown in Figure (i).

The conceptions of sustainability and ESD in the top left quadrant of Figure (i) are those in which experts would determine outcomes, which would then be prescribed to passive schools and their staff (see Chapter Three). The dominance of this authoritative and universal approach to ESD, in which educational authorities use their power over schools to expect all schools to do much the same thing, can result in big brother sustainability (see Figure (i)).

The bottom right quadrant is associated with bottom-up, grassroots approaches to sustainability and ESD (see Chapter Three) in which active citizens decide on local, more open outcomes. With such a participatory approach, each school decides what its most appropriate outcomes are. The grassroots sustainability that results requires educational authorities to devolve power to schools. Schools then devolve power to pupils.

The other two quadrants represent forms of ESD or sustainability characterised by limited openness and/or involvement. This can occur when pupils are encouraged to participate in activities that have been determined by others without the involvement of the pupils themselves. In these circumstances limited, token pupil participation or even non-participation (see

Table 2.1) might result. An example of this shallow interaction can occur when pupils become involved in a corporate sponsored recycling programme. While their involvement might provide these pupils with opportunities to consider recycling and develop a recycling action plan, they may not critically examine reducing consumption as part of this programme. An emphasis on the critical consideration of one or more of the four Rs: refuse, reduce, reuse, or repair might be a far more effective strategy for schools concerned with promoting sustainable lifestyles than a strategy that concentrates only on the fifth R: recycling.

An imposed environmental awareness approach may not engage critically in this discussion, let alone examine these other four forms of action. The environmental awareness approach to recycling may avoid critical, deeper engagement with the recycling issue. What results is 'feel good' sustainability, because the corporate sponsor is proud of its support of community recycling as this improves the company's image without it having to worry about challenges to the pursuit of economic growth. The pupils and their schools feel good because they have done something positive for the environment and perhaps raised some money for their school. The irony is that an approach that only encourages recycling may actually increase consumption: the more soft drinks you consume the more cans you can recycle. A more critical approach might be to consider reducing school consumption in addition to recycling, perhaps by reducing or refusing highly carbonated sugar rich drinks because of their possible detrimental effect on teeth. The consequence, ironically, might be to reduce the number of drink cans the school recycles.

Such initiatives may originate externally to schools. Drink vending machines in most Scottish schools only retail water and fruit juices as a result of changes in policy to promote healthy food consumption in schools a similar government policy driven initiative to promote the eating of healthy foods in schools will be introduced in England in 2006.

B: Conclusion

The central issue that confronts EE/ESD is to assist the development of sustainable societies, based on the principles of justice and equity, which reduce their environmental impact by living more lightly on the planet. These principles of justice and equity cannot be separated from questions of ecological sustainability (Elliot, 1999) or social and economic sustainability (see Figure 4.1).

Figure (i): A process based typology of sustainability (Based on Wals and Jickling, 2002)

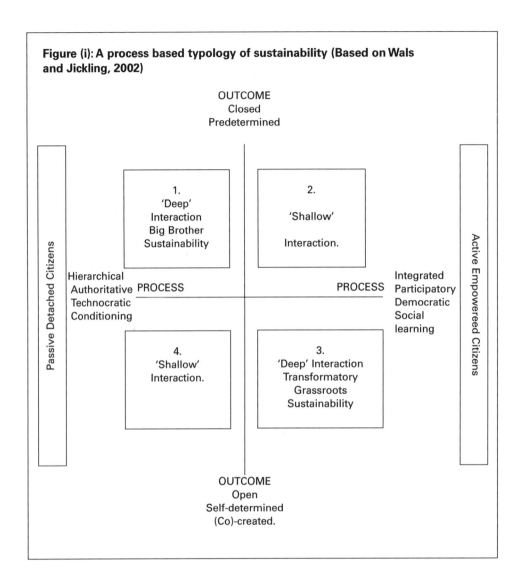

If EE/ESD describes an education concerned with the process of journeying towards sustainability and if the process is collaborative, participatory and contextualised does it really matter what such an education is called? For example do Jickling's (1992) objections to the use of educational terms that are for sustainability disappear if ESD/EfS is an education for process? Whatever the name, most definitions of educations linked with sustainability are united by their opposition to the narrow attainment focus associated with the school effectiveness movement and by their offers of transformatory alternatives. In the struggle for hearts and minds of educators, focusing on conceptions rather than labels would appear to be a more fruitful strategy than continually appearing to develop and topple slogans in the pursuit of claimed academic rigour. This debate about semantics is often capable of alienating school practitioners (Alexander, 1984; Leal Filho and Pace, 2002).

EE/ESD are the terms most frequently used in this book because they are the most common terms used in European countries. However in this book EE/ESD are used in the spirit of process-based collaborative, participatory whole school approaches that involve key concepts of school development, whole school approaches, self-evaluation, change and professional development. These concepts are examined in Section A which seeks to clarify these core concepts critically, Section B which focuses on case studies and Section C which looks at where schools can get support to develop whole school approaches. In reality, as most of the case studies in Section B show, the development of whole school approaches, while it should privilege participatory approaches, also requires some form of top-down support.

1

School improvement, school effectiveness or school development?

Christopher Bezzina and Paul Pace

Introduction

Concern for the improvement of education is widely evident today in practically all European countries. One major development in the present trend is that more emphasis is being directed at the school level, at the way schools function. Nations have wasted billions of Euros on many poorly conceived, but perhaps politically popular reforms, which in the end failed to produce any impact at the most critical level; the school, and learning and teaching. Similarly the energy and resources invested in EE and ESD projects over the years have had a relatively limited impact on educational systems. Reforms have frequently been proposed from outside the school community which were contradictory in nature, poorly implemented and had to be abandoned eventually or else left to die a natural death (Hopkins, 1987).

Any efforts to improve schools cannot be directed intelligently without understanding school dynamics. James Conant's advice given over thirty years ago that schools should be improved school by school is being re-echoed now by many educationalists (Elmore, 2002; Lambert, 1998). Understanding the dynamics of schools entails learning about the actions and influences of teachers, pupils, parents, community members and community organisations and the ways in which these influences operate and interact (Barth, 2002; Glickman, 2002). With its emphasis on empowering individuals to understand, interact with and improve their milieu, EE/ESD has proved to be an effective tool for promoting contextualised school development.

Such a perspective stresses the view that schools need to occupy a central position in educational discourse directed towards school improvement. In this context, teacher empowerment is seen as a powerful means and a crucial ingredient if schools are to improve (Fielding, 1995; West *et al*, 1995). Teachers occupy a critical role within the school community. Being the primary implementers of policy and the main intermediaries between pupils and school authorities, teachers are the hinges on which school improvement pivots. They are the meeting point, particularly through EE/ESD (Pace, 1996a), that could integrate traditional top-down management styles with bottom-up grassroots approaches to school management, based on pupil needs and interests (see Chapter Three).

One aim of this chapter is to set the scene and help promote the importance of a thorough understanding of the concept of school improvement. Making the effort to understand school improvement will help a school's staff to become more sensitive to the cultural and political underpinnings that such an exercise would entail if addressed strategically. A second aim is to identify those strategies that have been effective in school improvement across the very varied cultural and political contexts in which European schools operate so as to apply these methodologies in EE/ESD. There are at least two strands to school development identified in this chapter, a school effectiveness strand and a school improvement strand. These strands, while distinct, are not totally separate; they often interact and intertwine. This review commences by locating literature in its historical context; in one of three main phases of development the component stages of which are summarised in Figure 1.1. The literature within the last phase – the mid 1990s to the present – is then reviewed in greater depth.

The first phase of school improvement started to take shape as a distinct group of approaches and scholars/practitioners in the late 1970s and early 1980s (Potter *et al*, 2002). A project that characterised this first phase was the Organisation for Economic Co-operation and Development's (OECD) *International School Improvement Project* (ISIP) (Hopkins, 1987). Unfortunately many of the initiatives associated with this first phase of school improvement were 'free floating, rather than representing a systematic, programmatic and coherent approach to school change' (Potter *et al*, 2002: 244). The emphasis in this period was on individual schools and individual teacher's ownership of the change process, especially of organisational change and school self-evaluation. However, there was no significant conceptual or practical connection of these initiatives to pupil learning outcomes. Furthermore, these initiatives were variable and fragmented in conception and application and consequently, in the eyes of most school improvers and practitioners, most struggled to have an impact upon classroom practice (Reynolds, 1999). This general state of affairs was also evident in the mania to promote EE simply by ensuring the availability and dissemination of teaching packs and resources (Pace, 1996b) that followed the 1978 UNESCO Tbilisi Conference. Despite this somewhat negative analysis, Hopkins acknowledges that many of these studies initiated:

> .... widespread research into, and understanding of, the change process and the school as an organisation ... The studies highlighted the limitations of externally imposed changes, the importance of focussing on the school as the unit of change, and the need to take the change process seriously ... Similarly, the research on schools as organisations, demonstrated the importance of linking curriculum innovation to organisational change. (2001: 29)

The early 1990s gave rise to a second phase in the development of school improvement. This phase was characterised by the integration of various contributions from the school improvement and school effectiveness communities. A number of effectiveness and improvement researchers and practitioners had called for a fusion of approaches and insights (Hopkins *et al*, 1994; Gray *et al*, 1996) and this led to a merged perspective (Hopkins, Reynolds and Stoll as cited, in Gray *et al*, 1996). The same need to merge insights with methodology was the main theme of the Moscow International Congress on EE and Training (UNESCO-UNEP, 1988). The introduction of EE into schools had not been the 'bed of roses' it had originally seemed, mainly because it required a radical reconsideration of the rationales behind curricula and educational institutions; and a reorganisation of teaching methods (Booth, 1987). In an effort to put the development of EE/ESD back on track, the congress drew up its *International Strategy for Action in the Field of Environmental Education and Training for the 1990s* (Pace, 1996b). The school effectiveness tradition had made significant contributions to this new, merged intellectual enterprise, such as the value-added methodology for judging school success and for developing a large-scale, knowledge base about what works at school level to improve pupil outcomes (Teddlie and Reynolds, 2000).

The most recent, third stage of school improvement practice and philosophy, which started in the mid 1990s, attempts to draw lessons from contemporary improvement programmes and reforms. This approach is apparent in a number of school improvement programmes such as the *Improving the Quality of Education for All Project* (IQEA) (Hopkins, 2001), the

High Reliability Schools project (HRS) (Stringfield, 1995) and other projects. In Canada, this approach is evident in the various phases of work conducted in the Halton Board of Education (Stoll and Fink, 1996). In the Netherlands it manifests itself in the *Dutch National School Improvement Project* (Hopkins *et al*, 1994). The Sustainability Education in European Primary Schools Project (SEEPS) (Shallcross, 2004) adopts a similar approach to whole school development, in the field of EE/ESD (see Chapter Eleven).

Although there are significant variations amongst these programmes, these examples of third phase improvement initiatives demonstrate that there has been an enhanced focus upon the importance of pupil outcomes. Instead of the earlier emphasis upon improving processes, the focus is now upon seeing if these improvements are powerful enough to influence pupil outcomes. Focusing on the importance of the process of improvement has not been shelved, but a mixed method orientation has been adopted in which data on quantitative outcomes and qualitative processes are used to measure educational quality. Mixed methods will include audits of existing classroom and school processes, their outcomes, and comparisons with desired end states (see Chapters Three and Four), in particular the educational experiences of different pupil groups (Potter *et al*, 2002).

An increased concern to ensure that improvement programmes relate to and impact upon practitioners and practices through using increasingly sophisticated training, coaching and development programmes has increased consciousness of the importance of capacity building. This increasing awareness of capacity building includes not only staff development but also medium-term strategic planning, change strategies that utilise pressure and support and the intelligent use of external support agencies (Stoll and Fink, 1996) (see Chapter Four and Chapter Ten). This third phase of school improvement also brings with it an appreciation of the importance of cultural change in embedding and sustaining school improvement. There has also been more emphasis on a careful balance between vision building and adapting structures to support these aspirations (see Chapter Four).

Having outlined the recent historical contexts that have contributed towards the evolution of contemporary thinking about school improvement, our focus shifts to a review of the latest research literature relating to strategies used to implement successful school improvement programmes. This literature is particularly relevant to this book as it identifies the factors that need to be explored and nurtured to achieve improvement, as well as providing a backdrop for the adoption of whole school approaches to promote EE/ESD, which will be discussed in subsequent chapters.

Figure 1.1: The historical development of research literature in school development

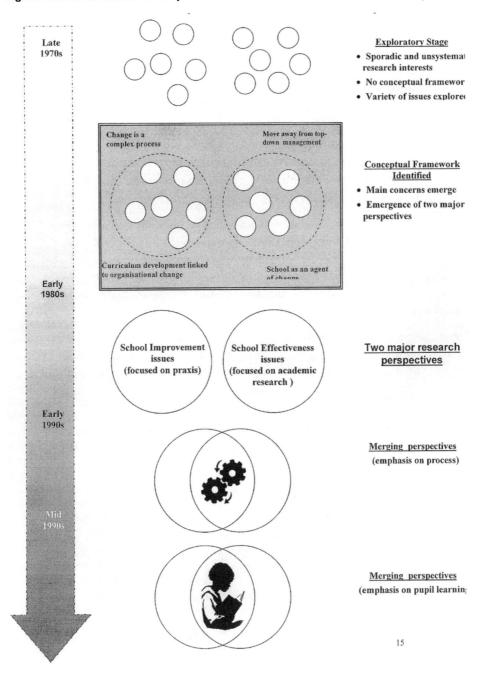

Strategies for improving schools

Most of the material reviewed here refers to processes managed from within the school (Stoll and Fink, 1996) and targeted at both pupil achievement and the school's ability to manage change (Ainscow *et al*, 1994); a simultaneous focus on outcomes and processes. In this context, improvement is seen as a sustained upward trend in effectiveness. An improving school is considered to be one that increases its effectiveness over time, that is, it increases added value for pupils over successive cohorts. All the authors cited stress the self-managing nature of the improving school. Schools are most effective when they are aided from time to time by external support and take control of an externally determined agenda and rule, rather than become the objects of change. Caldwell and Spinks define the self-managing school as:

> .... a system of education to which there has been decentralised a significant amount of authority and responsibility to make decisions about the allocation of resources within a centrally determined framework of goals, policies, standards and accountabilities. Resources are defined broadly to include knowledge, technology, power, material, people, time, assessment, information and finance. (1988: 4-5)

When schools are empowered by the right mix of autonomy and support, they have better prospects for improvement. Researchers have been looking for similarities among schools that have been running successful school improvement programmes to produce lists of what works in school improvement. Harris (2002) conducted a broad comparative analysis of highly successful school improvement programmes and demonstrated a number of shared principles or features. This analysis found that effective school improvement programmes:

- focus closely on classroom improvement
- utilise discrete instructional or pedagogical strategies, that is they are explicit about the models of teaching they prescribe
- apply pressure at the implementation stage to ensure adherence to the programme
- collect systematic evaluative evidence about the impact upon schools and classrooms
- mobilise change at a number of levels within the organisation, (for example, classroom, department, teacher level)
- generate cultural as well as structural change
- engage teachers in professional dialogue and development
- provide external agency and support

16

This comparative study showed that while the school improvement programmes and projects evaluated varied in terms of content, nature and approach they reflected a similar philosophy. Central to this philosophy was the idea that the school was the centre of change and the teacher was the catalyst for classroom change and development. Within these highly effective school improvement programmes, the non-negotiable elements were a focus on teaching and learning, a commitment to professional development and diffused, devolved or distributed leadership (Gronn, 2002). In their extensive analysis of school improvement literature and of 25 successful world-wide school improvement programmes, Potter *et al*, (2002) showed that there are a certain number of general leadership strategies behind effective improvement programmes:

- having a vision: since without a concept of where we are trying to get to, the verb to improve has no meaning
- monitoring: we must know where we are now in relation to the vision
- planning: how will we get from where we are, to where we want to be
- using performance indicators: to track progress in the aspects we monitor

Other research (Ainscow *et al*, 1994; Gray *et al*, 1999) indicates that, regardless of the type of school, there are certain internal preconditions for successful improvement to occur. These include a school-wide emphasis on teaching and learning, a commitment to staff development and training and the use of performance data to guide decisions, targets and tactics. In addition they identify the importance of teamwork both within staff groups (collaborative planning, effective communication) and with stakeholders (involvement of teachers, pupils and parents in decision-making) and the need for time and resources for reflection and research.

Practitioners such as local education authorities (LEAs) have also attempted to ascertain the most important features of successful school improvement programmes. For example, Birmingham LEA in the UK, in it efforts to improve schools, identified seven processes that became the focus of their school improvement programmes (Brighouse and Woods, 1999: 11):

- practice of teaching and learning
- exercise of leadership
- practice of management and organisation
- practice of collective review

- creation of the environment most suitable for learning
- promotion of staff development
- encouragement of parental and community involvement

Leadership strategies for schools facing challenging circumstances

The literature reviewed so far has outlined some of the more commonly occurring characteristics of successful school improvement projects. The literature suggests that many of the principles governing effective improvement are universal, with little reference made to context specificity (Teddlie and Reynolds, 2000). There are certain principles that have been particularly associated with successful improvement programmes implemented by schools facing challenging circumstances. The literature indicates that schools that succeed in improving against a background of significant pupil and community disadvantage (National Commission of Education, 1996) share the following characteristics:

- a leadership stance that embodies and builds a team approach
- a vision of success that includes a view of how to improve
- the careful use of targets
- the improvement of the physical environment
- possessing common expectations about behaviour and success
- an investment in good relations with parents and the community

A more recent study carried out for the English National College for School Leadership (Harris and Chapman, 2002) came up with a number of recommended strategies that leaders of schools in challenging circumstances could adopt to improve their schools. These strategies are grouped into eight areas:

- focus on learning and teaching
- generating positive relationships
- providing a clear vision and high expectations
- improving the environment
- providing time and opportunities for collaboration
- distributing leadership: building teams
- engaging the community
- evaluating and innovating

Given the literature surveyed so far and the aims of this chapter we will focus on three main features of school improvement: leaders and leadership, capacity building and staff development and collective review.

Leaders and leadership

Birmingham LEA in the UK believes that the core purpose of the head-teacher is:

> .... to provide professional leadership for a school, which secures its success and improvement, ensuring high quality education for all its pupils and improved standards of learning and achievement. The headteacher provides vision, leadership and direction for the school and ensures that it is managed and organised to meet its aims and targets. (Brighouse, 2000)

Traditional views of leaders as special people who set the direction, make the key decisions, and energise the troops are deeply rooted in an individualistic and nonsystemic world-view (Senge, 1990) and in an heroic concept of the leader. So long as such myths prevail, they reinforce a focus on short-term events and charismatic heroes rather than on systemic forces and collective learning. The contemporary view of effective school leaders, which has moved on since the early 1990s, is summed up by Riley and MacBeath:

> .... effective' school leaders are distinguished by their vision and passion and by their capacity to bring a critical spirit into the complex and demanding job of headship, whilst at the same time focusing on staff and pupil performance and on classroom pedagogy. (1998:151)

Recent research (Court, 2003; Kimber, 2003) highlights a core of strongly held and enacted values that are the key to successful headship. Through a series of case studies Gold *et al*, (2003) found principals who held 'a number of clear – and shared – educational values and beliefs. They were principled indivi-duals with a strong commitment to their 'mission', determined to do the best for their schools, particularly for the pupils and students within them' (136). It is interesting that the values manifested by successful headteachers were broadly 'social democratic or liberal humanist in nature' (Gold *et al*, 2003: 136) and were concerned with issues like inclusion, equal opportunities, high expectations, cooperation, teamwork, commitment, understanding, and the engagement of stakeholders. Related to these values were the personal quali-ties of school leaders. These included openness, accessibility, compassion, honesty, integrity, consistency, risk-taking and awareness of others (Bezzina, 1999; Duignan, 1998). An important piece of evidence that the Gold *et al*, (2003) studies have identified is that value-driven leadership is embodied in particular ways of operating within schools. The current drive is towards a more collaborative style of leadership, one which contemporary literature describes as distributed leadership (Gronn, 2000).

Leadership is probably best conceived as a group quality, as a set of functions which must be carried out by the group, sometimes including pupils, and that it could either be concentrated, monopolised and focused or instead dispersed, shared and distributed. If viewed from this perspective, leadership is not seen as coming from one person and going to another following the dualism model of leader-follower. Instead leadership emphasises the fluidity of circumstances. This represents an interactional, constructivist standpoint and helps us to appreciate leadership as a fluid and emergent phenomenon rather than being fixed.

Du Quesnay (2003) believes the key to successful school management is to distribute responsibility among staff:

> .... it's about building people's confidence and sense of value to the school. When you walk into a school where it happens – and there are too many where it doesn't – you can feel the buzz in the atmosphere. (2003: 11)

One way of adding a sense of value to the school is to nurture a shared vision among the school's stakeholders, including pupils, since this can provide the focus and energy for learning:

> .... today, 'vision' is a familiar concept in corporate leadership. But when you look carefully you find that most 'visions' are one person's (or one group's) vision imposed on an organisation. Such visions, at best, command compliance – not commitment. A shared vision is a vision that many people are truly committed to, because it reflects their own personal vision. (Senge, 1990: 206)

However, an effective school leader must be able to promote an environment that translates this shared vision into day-to-day practices:

> .... having vision alone is of course, not sufficient ... School leaders must gain the commitment of others to that vision, and then ensure that it shapes the policies, plans and day-to-day activities in the school. (Caldwell and Spinks, 1988: 174)

A shared vision translates itself into day-to-day practice through effective strategic planning and operational target setting (Davies and Ellison, 1999). This is the basic principle found at the heart of the very successful Eco-Schools programme, managed by the Foundation for Environmental Education (FEE) (see Chapter Eleven), which seeks to promote EE/ESD through whole school approaches. The programme promotes a plan of action that systematically weaves EE/ESD principles into a school's management policy so that the whole school community progressively incorporates an environmental ethic within its school ethos. Day *et al*, (2001) go further in arguing that a school leader's vision is continually tested by difficult day-to-day decisions:

> .... continuing poor teaching by a member of staff, for example, creates a leadership dilemma, cutting across the headteachers' personal framework of values and beliefs, their ideological and educative commitments to the development of everyone in the school community. Engaging in dismissal procedures touches upon the culture of the school, staff morale, and the nature of the relationship between leader and led. (p31)

They also stress that successful headteachers do not shrink from taking such tough decisions, illustrating the clear if painful boundary that must be drawn at key times between the personal and professional relationships which are at the heart of the educational health of school communities.

Capacity building

A widely accepted definition of capacity building is 'the collective competency of the school as an entity to bring about effective change' (Harvey, 2003: 21). This implies that schools need to adopt a collaborative culture, which draws upon the full range of professional skills and expertise to be found in the organisation (Fullan and Hargreaves, 1992). Such management cultures move away from the individuality that characterised the last generation of schools and was heavily dependent on the headteacher as the leader, towards the high-performing organisation distinguished by teams in which each member is a 'self-led, growing and dynamic individual prepared to contribute to the greater good of the team and the organisation' (Sawatzki, 1997: 147). In other words, within the context of school improvement, capacity is the ability to enable all students to reach higher standards and actively contribute to school development.

Capacity may be built by improving the performance of teachers, adding more resources, materials or technology and by restructuring how tasks are undertaken (Harris, 2002: 51). It may also require a new ideology of pupils from passive consumers of what the school has to offer to active stakeholders in the identification, implementation and evaluation of the school's vision (John, 1996). Such an ideological change will obviously influence the ways in which teaching and learning occur. Because of their focus on action and whole school development EE and ESD provide a context for the school community to develop these characteristics in a planned and sustained manner.

Research commissioned by the English National College for School Leadership into capacity building (Hadfield *et al*, 2002) revealed divergent perspectives between theorists and practitioners on capacity building. When describing their own approach to leadership and building capacity, headteachers found Stoll's action-orientated principles (Stoll and Fink, 1996) among the most useful. These include: challenging expectations, establishing a positive climate, working between and beyond schools, managing structures, broadening leadership and listening, especially to pupils.

Another factor that increases a school's capacity for improvement is relative stability within the senior management team. Howson (2003) investigated the relationship in primary and secondary schools in England between a headteacher's length of service and selected PANDA[1] grades of his/her school. This analysis revealed a clear positive association between these two variables. A and A* rated schools had the highest percentage of headteachers with a length of service of over six years and E and E* schools had the smallest percentage. This study reinforces the argument that school leaders need to be in place for a number of years to see that their own and others' ideas are introduced, nurtured and translated into practice; that they become culture bearers as well as culture founders (Nias *et al*, 1989) in their schools (see Chapter Six).

Staff development and collective review
School improvement is ultimately about the enhancement of pupils' progress, development and achievement. It is not surprising that most research evidence indicates how important teacher development is to school development. Schools that are successful facilitate the learning of both pupils and teachers (Fullan, 1992; Harris, 2002) and the quality of professional development so that learning becomes an essential component of interventions that lead to successful school improvement. Collaborative relations and collective learning are at the core of building the capacity for school improvement. This implies a particular form of teacher development that extends teaching repertoires and engages teachers in changing their practices (Hopkins and Harris, 1997). Highly successful school improvement projects reflect a form of teacher development that concentrates upon and goes beyond the enhancement of teaching skills, knowledge and competence. It involves teachers in an exploration of different approaches to teaching and learning that seek to empower pupils to take an active part in their learning and to adopt a participatory approach to school life (see Chapter Two).

Despite this research evidence and the range of centralised professional development programmes (see Chapter Four) in the UK and elsewhere, the impact of such programmes upon classroom practice remains variable. The traditional centralised delivery model of professional development has been a topic of substantial debate over recent years, leading to a series of problems (see Table 4.4), collectively described as the theory-practice divide. As Hoban and Erickson (2004) argue, many continuing professional development (CPD) programmes seem to lack any systematic design for learning as a focus for their activities. Fullan (1995) argues that:

> .... professional development for teachers has a poor track record because it lacks a theoretical base and coherent focus. On the one hand, professional development is treated as a vague panacea ... on the other hand, professional development is defined too narrowly and becomes artificially detached from 'real-time' learning. It becomes the workshop, or possibly an ongoing series of professional development sessions. In either case, it fails to have a sustained cumulative impact. (253)

Other researchers have concurred about the inadequacy of traditional inservice training (INSET) to promote sustained professional learning (Bezzina, 2002; Surgrue, 2002). There is evidence to show that many inservice training programmes fail to change teaching behaviours (Fullan, 1991). The difference between CPD and INSET is subtle and not always understood by teachers. Whilst all educators need to be involved in both CPD and INSET, it is CPD that determines the effects that INSET may have on adult or pupil learning.

School staff undertake INSET whilst in post. This can entail attending courses in particular curriculum areas, in management development for those staff with special responsibilities or areas of educational expertise that staff may need to develop to realise high quality curriculum provision. A special educational needs co-ordinator (SENCO), for example, will need to keep abreast of developments in his/her specialist curriculum area, just as other subject coordinators will want to be informed about current practice and development in their curriculum areas. INSET can also be undertaken by a whole school where it is appropriate for the staff to receive training in specific areas such as behaviour management, developing a school discipline policy or information and communications technology (ICT). INSET can also be a shared experience for a cluster of schools in the same location.

CPD has a broader sweep and can address issues such as leadership, developing management strategies, whole school development, educational ethics or philosophies. Using CPD to circulate new research findings gives teachers the opportunity to develop an evidence-based understanding of pedagogy. CPD may demand a higher order of thinking in order to develop the creativity that will be reflected in the classroom as teachers become more aware of the jobs they are doing. In this way the professional role of teachers can be embraced and used to raise self-esteem and morale amongst school staff. CPD and INSET are important aspects of the development of teachers' skills and abilities and are increasingly being merged into a conglomerate in which the term CPD means staff training as well as professional development.

The following quotation describes the importance of education for practising teachers and the difference between the terms CPD and INSET:

> .... change in the classroom, which involves more than extending the repertoire by acquiring new skills will mean changing attitudes, beliefs and personal theories and reconstructing a personal approach to teaching. INSET therefore needs to provide new experiences, support the anxieties which accompany not just the threat but the genuine difficulties of change and give people time to reflect, work things out and think things through. (Joyce and Showers, 1995: 13)

Staff development will never have its intended impact as long as it is grafted on to schools in the form of discrete, unconnected projects. 'The closer one gets to the culture of schools and the professional lives of teachers, the more complex and daunting the reform agenda becomes' (Fullan, 1992: 111). Harris (2002) argues that one of the limitations of traditional in-service training within schools is the lack of ongoing support once the training day is over. Improving this position implies changing the way in which staff development is organised in most schools. In particular, this means 'establishing opportunities for immediate and sustained practice, classroom observation, collaboration and peer coaching' (Harris, 2002: 100).

The literature points towards the centrality of collaborative enquiry and reflective practice in the school improvement process. MacBeath (1988: 9) argues that 'as in many other professions, the commitment to critical and systematic reflection on practice as a basis for individual and collective development is at the heart of what it means to be a professional teacher.' Costa and Kallick (2000: 60) suggest that 'every school's goal should be to habituate reflection throughout the organisation individually and collectively, with teachers, students, and the school community.' Reflective organisations are places where people can bring themselves wholeheartedly to work. Schall (1995: 207) maintains that 'being fully present at work is a remarkable and powerful experience; all the more so if one contrasts it experientially with its opposite, disconnection or alienation.' One powerful way in which teachers are encouraged to reflect upon and improve their practice is through a process of enquiry, a means by which they can consider their work in a critical way. It has been suggested (York-Barr *et al*, 2001) that engaging in school-based enquiry is an essential element of the teacher's role. Enquiry and reflection are expected of teachers as part of their professional learning and development.

A school-focused teacher education programme that addresses all the features outlined above was developed in the SEEPS project (Shallcross, 2004). The project seeks to disseminate EE/ESD by promoting whole school approaches. The programme repeatedly encourages teachers to reflect critically on their practice and their school's management systems and to become active agents for change within their school and its community, partly through their own personal development.

If schools are serious about improvement, the centrality of teacher development in this process needs to be recognised. For authentic improvement to take place, all stakeholders need to be involved and engaged. School improvement is at heart a collective activity where organisational learning is a dynamic and systemic process (Harris, 2002: 100). As Wenger (1999: 262) notes, the focus is 'not on knowledge as an accumulated commodity but on learning as a social system productive of new meanings'. Schools that improve become learning communities that generate the capacity and capability to sustain that improvement. They are 'communities of practice' (Sergiovanni, 2000: 140) which provide a context for collaboration and the generation of shared meaning. 'Such communities hold the key to transformation – the kind that has real effects on people's lives' (Wenger 1999: 85).

This empowerment brings about changes not only in practice in learning and teaching but also in the values, attitudes and beliefs that ultimately influence what teachers and other school staff do in schools on a daily basis. These changes apply to teachers in a class relating to pupils, as well as to teachers or support staff relating to other colleagues (see Chaplin, 1996). If teacher empowerment is utilised appropriately, members of staff will slowly begin to feel that they are respected and valued as individuals who can contribute in meaningful ways to school improvement. It is a slow process that can be gruelling at times, with its ups and downs, but it is a journey worth pursuing (Bezzina and Pace, 2004).

In this introductory chapter we have not gone into detail about the notion of school development. We have focused on the importance of school improvement and the understanding that for this to take place we need to create school development initiatives. We emphasised the need to see improvement and hence school development as a process by which the members of an institution develop the capacity to reflect on the nature and purpose of their work together. In this context, school development relates change with purpose, makes prevailing beliefs, values and norms of the school community explicit. This is what is essentially behind school development practices. They deal with growth between and among people in a specific group or school community.

In this context, and the development of this book, it may be useful to consider the main differences between school effectiveness, improvement and development. This will help the reader to note how areas such as EE/ESD have a direct impact on school life and pupils' education in particular. Table 1.1 is intended to illustrate some differences in emphasis between school development, school effectiveness and school improvement, not to suggest oppositional, either/or differences between these approaches to school change, for such a position would be untenable.

Table 1.1: School development and some key differences between school effectiveness and school improvement (Based on Capra, 1996 adapted by Shallcross, 2003).

	School effectiveness	School improvement
Focus	**Pupil attainment**	**Pupil achievement**
Learning focuses on	Outcomes	Processes
Curriculum	Subject based	Thematic/holistic
Control	External and hierarchical	Internal, participatory and collaborative
Schools and their staffs	Accountable for their actions	Responsible for their actions
Evaluation and comparison of schools through	Standardisation	Quality standards linked to self-evaluation
Most highly valued quality	Rationality	Intuition
The key driver of the system	Competition within and between schools	Cooperation within and between schools
The core intellectual skill	Analysis	Synthesis
Schools	Mechanistic organisations (see Table 5.4)	Organic organisations (see Table 5. 4)

While learning processes may be privileged, they cannot take place in a vacuum. They need content and outcomes in order to function, indeed learning processes themselves can be seen as outcomes. Equally, as will be emphasised in many chapters of this book, school development and EE/ESD are not anti-attainment stances but part of the educational movement to privilege pupil achievement in European schools. One thrust of this argument is that much case study evidence indicates that when schools focus on pupil achievement, as is the case in whole school development, attainment improves by comparison with similar schools that do not adopt such an approach. As this chapter shows, the second and third stages of school development are based on a synthesis of the emphases outlined in Table 1.1.

Chapter Four presents the argument that schools adopting whole school approaches in EE/ESD should initially demonstrate how they are successfully meeting the standardised outcomes of the testing frequently used to judge school effectiveness. Some of the evidence to support this argument comes from quantifiable standards that are used to assess school effectiveness.

School development is therefore a process whereby a self-reflective community increases the effectiveness of learning and teaching in its community through a commitment to the notions of collaboration, task culture, data gathering and mutual accountability (Bezzina, 1988). By taking responsibility for their own development and having a clearly delineated sequence of changes to follow, schools can maximise their use of resources while creating the kind of climate best suited to their pupils. Furthermore, school development guarantees a form of continuous self-renewal and progressive adaptation (see Chapter Three).

Conclusion

This chapter has outlined the features of successful attempts to develop and improve schools and introduced themes that will be explored in the book. It has drawn some general conclusions about the core principles that should underpin school improvement, such as ownership of the process of improvement, and has examined the evidence about what worked in different kinds of school.

The literature stresses that given the right preconditions, improvement strategies and programmes can be relevant to all kinds of schools, even those facing challenging circumstances, notwithstanding the differences between these schools. But the focus of the various initiatives and the order of implementation of the various components clearly needs to vary according to the precise context, environment and conditions of each school. Teacher empowerment has been emphasised as central to school development. The learning environment that can take the individual and institution forward requires commitment that will necessitate 'not only turning to something but also turning from something' (Bezzina and Pace, 2004: 52).

2

Whole school approaches, forging links and closing gaps between knowledge, values and actions

Tony Shallcross

Introduction

> Coming here today, I have no hidden agenda. I am fighting for my future. ... At school you teach us to behave in the world. You teach us not to fight with others, to work things out, to respect others, to clean up our mess, not to hurt other creatures, to share and not be greedy. Then why do you go out and do those things you teach us not to do? (Severn Cullis-Suzuki, age 12, addressing the Rio Earth Summit, 1992, Eden Project, 2004: 99-100)

This quotation summarises the main problem schools face in addressing sustainable development[2]; the need to practise what they teach. In order to promote sustainable actions schools need to become active agents of change rather than passive transmitters of information and/or values (Uzzell *et al*, 1994). Whole school approaches are one way in which schools can become such agents of social and environmental change. A key feature of school agency is school democracy (Aspin, 1995; Beane and Apple, 1999) which grants power to pupils and adults to make decisions and act on these decisions. This is democracy in the participative sense that can be implemented in schools through participation and active citizenship (DfEE and QCA, 1999), not democracy confined to voting and representation.

Schools have a crucial role in helping children to play their part in democracy (Council of Europe, 1999). Active citizenship needs to be founded on notions of children's rights and responsibilities and rooted in actions that are authentic because they relate to real issues arising in schools and their local communities (Uzzell, 1999). This chapter outlines a vision of what whole school approaches entail, outlines a design for whole school approaches and explains why these approaches can make an important contribution to EE or ESD.[3]

The issue

The UN Secretary General regards sustainable development as the biggest challenge facing humanity in the 21st Century. The 2005 G8 Summit recognised climate change as the most serious problem facing the planet. Many scientists believe that increases in atmospheric carbon dioxide levels caused by human activities, such as the burning of fossil fuels and deforestation, are responsible for planetary warming. So the environmental crisis is social not natural. It arises largely because modern society's concept of community is truncated (O'Sullivan, 1999). European moral theories have generally taken it for granted that the interests of humanity take precedence over those of other lifeforms. Consequently Western societies do not usually give plants, animals and the natural systems that support them due moral consideration when deciding on actions that affect the natural environment. However, even when humanity understands the threats posed by environmental problems such as climate change, it often fails to react or reacts too slowly to resolve them.

However, as religious observance and traditional communities decline in many European countries, the moral role of schools as potential centres of community change is more important than it has been for a significant period (Fullan and Hargreaves, 1992). So how do schools become centres of sustainable community action and thus help to broaden pupils' understanding of community to encompass nature?

Actions are not entirely controlled by personal preference or individual agency. The social and economic pressures that people are under to consume are evident from the emphasis on advertising in the European media. Branding sends the message that we are not only what we eat but what we buy. In this culture of consumerism, economic and political systems rarely advocate or facilitate alternative lifestyles that reduce human consumption. Instead, the emphasis tends to be on developing technologies and patterns of purchasing that will maintain consumption levels while reducing their environmental impact. The decision at the 2005 G8 summit to shun targets for the reduction of atmospheric carbon dioxide in favour of supporting technologies that offer boundless energy at lower environmental cost per unit is indicative of this approach.

Although most descriptions of EE/ESD, from the first UNESCO conference on EE in Tblisi in 1978 to the United Nations Strategy for the Decade of ESD (UN DESD, 2005-2014), seek to promote the change to more environmentally friendly lifestyles, education may actually be part of the problem. The mistaken assumption still exists that if people learn about environmental problems they will act for their resolution (Sterling, 2001). Yet even when people support environmental changes they frequently lack the range of skills necessary to make these changes (Uzzell *et al*, 1994). So while knowledge and positive attitudes to environmental issues are necessary these have not been sufficient to promote the change to more sustainable actions on a societal scale. Until relatively recently education has been driven by an ideology of childhood that considers pupils to be citizens in waiting rather than present citizens (Alderson, 2000), it has not treated children as equal and responsible partners in the process of change. Modern education generally subscribes to this conventional ideology of childhood that assumes that children are minors, passive receivers of knowledge who are under the hierarchical influence of adults. Consequently, although environmental concerns have high priority for young people, many feel powerless to act on these concerns as no one will listen to their ideas about environmental change (Freeman, 1999).

Another difficulty in EE/ESD can be the focus on environmental problems. While education should not seek to make pupils feel personally responsible for the environmental crisis, apathy can result if schooling focuses on apparently intractable environmental problems, because they appear to be caused by governments and/or large corporations. Children, like other people, become depressed if they cannot change what happens to them, which can lead them to give up even in situations where they can make a difference. So, not only do schools fail to prepare pupils for the future, they can undermine the personal worth children need for the continued self-development (Bandura, 1986) that can lead to sustainable actions. A further problem for EE/ESD is that modern education is associated with personal advancement and the promotion of economic growth. Is it a coincidence that many European nations, with some of the world's highest levels of education, are responsible for much of the planet's environmental degradation? Is education partly a cause of the environmental crisis?

How can whole school approaches provide an answer?

The rediscovery and extension of community to include the natural world combined with greater attention to *active* citizenship in education may redress the educational problems outlined above. However, debates about community-focused citizenship education, EE or ESD often distinguish between process and outcomes. The danger with focusing on outcomes alone is that this approach splits theory from practice and regards citizenship as an amalgam of facts taught to pupils by teachers, not as the social interactions that pupils encounter in schools (Alderson, 2000). A focus on process in EE/ESD is crucial because we do not as yet fully understand what sustainable development looks like and even when we think we understand sustainable development, sustainable solutions will differ from one community and context to another. By focusing on processes, on how societies educate their young generation, education can empower pupils by equipping them with the skills they need to assist schools, themselves and their local communities to become more sustainable. Whole school approaches that focus on educational processes such as participation and collaboration offer one very attractive way of closing the gaps between knowledge, attitudes and actions in EE/ESD.

In simple terms whole schools approaches mean that schools practise what they teach by trying to minimise the gaps between the values they profess and those values implicit in their actions (Posch, 1993). They seek to integrate all aspects of school life by making links between the formal curriculum; what happens in classrooms and the non-formal curriculum; what happens in other aspects of school and community life that have an influence on learning (see Figure 2.1). Such approaches integrate teaching and learning with the social/organisational and technical/economic aspects of school practice (Posch, 1999). If the formal curriculum addresses climate change how is this concern reflected in the way in which energy is used in schools? If curriculum guidelines include active citizenship how are pupils encouraged to participate in deciding and implementing sustainable actions in their schools? Whole school approaches are education as a way of life: they are approaches in which schools become a microcosm of a sustainable rather than an unsustainable society (Sterling, 2001). These approaches involve processes of development that shape human intellectual, physical, geographical, social and emotional relationships with the environment to achieve sustainable lifestyles for all (Posch, 1999). The socio-organisational strand in Figure 2.1 is arguably the key to whole school approaches because it promotes the participation and collaboration that lead to the other strands not only being addressed but integrated with each other.

Whole school approaches are not just the preserve of teachers, they involve pupils, parents, carers and all those who manage the infrastructure of schools and the services schools offer to support education, such as catering, energy and estate management. Thus EE/ESD has to transform not only the content and processes of the formal curriculum and the purposes of learning but also the ways in which educational institutions and educational buildings work (Orr, 1994). But these changes will only come about if people think critically about values, participate in decisions and understand their consequences. Evaluation is also included in any model of whole school approaches as it is integral to a plan-do-review cycle in schools (see Figure 2.1). After all most proposals for educational change are responses to someone's evaluative critique of current provision.

EE/ESD is committed to sustainable actions but what does the word action mean? Action is the continuous flow of conduct (Argyris and Schön, 1996), of actual interventions, that should not be confused with behavioural change that occurs in a direction determined by somebody else (Uzzell *et al*, 1994). Some describe action as intentional and behaviours, such as coughing, as instinctive (Schnack, 1998). However, this distinction between the instinctive and intentional misses the crucial notion of culturally intuitive actions such as covering my face when I sneeze. This is not an example of an instinctive response to a stimulus but a culturally and contextually shaped action that we do not consciously consider before performing. Through learning that is contextually situated, many socially and environmentally sustainable acts can become culturally intuitive, second nature actions. But these acts

Figure 2.1: The five strands of a whole school approach to EE/ESD (Shallcross, 2003)

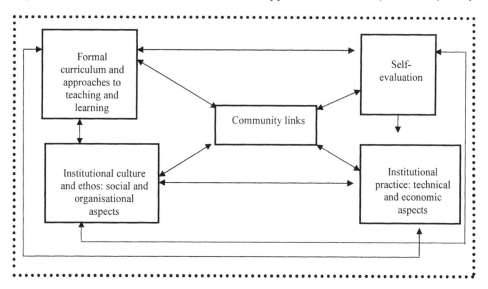

33

will only become widespread and second nature if they are reinforced by seeing what is learned in the classroom being applied in the non-formal curriculum, in the routine daily life of the school. Such integration is often apparent in the mutual care that is apparent in the actions of pupils and adults in many schools. Such caring does not just result from considered rational actions: many of these acts of caring are second nature. The crucial thing is that these actions have been learned in schools, often through the non-formal curriculum

Actions (see Figure 2.2) can be individual or collective, direct when people plant trees or indirect when people seek to influence others, by writing that advocates alternative, sustainable lifestyles. Actions can also be divided into political, those which are intended to influence others and personal, those which we do for ourselves. While knowledge leading to direct action is critical in the promotion of sustainable lifestyles it is not necessarily superior to knowledge that only promotes reflection (Clover, 2002). Sustainable lifestyles are not just about recycling, especially if such recycling results from authoritative interventions from outside or within schools which limit the participation of children (see Introduction). Reflective knowledge may sow seeds in childhood that blossom directly into sustainable actions in the future.

Although not all sustainable actions need be direct, sustainable lifestyles will only happen when substantial societal changes are made through direct sustainable actions. But privileging direct over indirect action may also have a social bias, most Europeans on limited incomes may not be able to afford organic food. It is inappropriate for schools to advocate actions, such as re-cycling, unless pupils and staff have the capability to perform these actions – saying that people ought to do something implies that they can (Des Jardins, 1993). It is those societies, individuals and schools whose actions contribute most to the environmental crisis that need to make the biggest shifts in developing personal, organisational and societal capacity for direct sustainable actions.

Local actions have authenticity because they are usually directed at real issues and decided by those who intend to implement them (Jensen, 2002). Conserving energy, developing school grounds or supporting local old people are more tangible and immediate for pupils in European schools than learning about the deforestation of the Amazon Basin. Not that the problems of planetary deforestation should be ignored, but simply that for most people their close locality is their most significant action field

Figure 2.2: Four types of environmental action (Jensen, 2002)

	Direct	Indirect
Individual	1	2
Collective	3	4

(Vognsen, 1995). Humans may also be genetically hot wired for local action because of their powerful emotional commitment to what is socially, spatially and temporally immediate (Wilson, 2002). Often a local crisis such as environmental vandalism or the death of a pupil has become a driver for whole school development (Shallcross, 2004).

Authentic community links involve interpersonal, interagency and inter-school networks (Uzzell, *et al*, 1994). However, local community based actions are most effective when they are linked with knowledge about wider, regional and planetary socio-economic and environmental issues (see Chapters Six and Ten). Thinking globally must relate to school practice, this is why EE and ESD have made working through the near environment a virtue. Some argue that EE/ESD which is not applied beyond the school gates is not authentic (Elliot, 1999; Posch, 1999).

However, emphasising local action can sometimes raise problems for schools. It can be difficult to see what is near, precisely because it is so well known and ordinary. Under these circumstances the art of teaching is to help pupils to see the ordinary as extraordinary. But working with highly contro-versial local issues, such as discussing over-fishing in a school in a fishing community (Schnack, 1998), can be difficult if these issues create friction and conflict with parents, local citizens and/or politicians because the emo-tional immediacy of the issue disrupts considered judgment.

Conversely, the separation of environmental knowledge in formal curricula from sustainable actions in non-formal curricula and local communities socialises hypocrisy (Shallcross, 2003). Pupils come to accept that expressing concern about the environment while failing to introduce sustainable practices is normal adult action. Whole school approaches by modelling sustainable lifestyles (UNESCO, 2004) become a socialising process which can break this cycle. The continuity of social relationships in whole school approaches not only reduces this tendency, it also increases mutual trust and leads to cooperation (Ridley, 1996). By belonging to a functioning social community pupils become agents of change (Uzzell *et al*, 1994). If pupils decide to make their school litter free it becomes easier to persuade potential litterers not to litter because their conduct would be seen as socially unacceptable. But if littering goes unchallenged, social pressure diminishes and littering may increase (Clayton and Radcliffe, 1996).

Action is also important in EE/ESD because it reduces the sense of powerlessness as learning and action proceed together and strengthen the commitment to sustainable practices. This is a bottom-up approach that respects democratic values more than a top-down prescriptive approach. Values education in whole school approaches is not a passive process concerned with imposing predetermined attitudes but a dynamic process in which values are caught rather than taught through engagement with decision-making and action. Through whole school approaches, ethical education rooted in democracy and cooperative relationships between communities, teachers, parents and pupils can begin at an early age (Farrer with Hawkes, 2000). Pupils learn to respect each other, to cooperate, to listen and discuss – all attributes essential to a true working democracy (Brain, 2001). The personal commitment to sustainable actions is promoted if habits are established early in life when the most effective routine practices often appear least obtrusive (Giddens, 1979). In whole school approaches pupils accept these practices as second nature because they are integral to the school's culture.

However, it is crucial that such practices are not thwarted by the non-formal curriculum. The social, economic and environmental strands of sustainable development need to be integrated not only with formal learning and teaching but also with other school practices (Figure 2.1). This does not just involve changing from a fragmented to an integrated view of knowledge, it has to connect pupils' experiences of school and community to form a web of coherent experiences. In this way schools become communities of practice (Wenger, 1999) in which people learn how to act by participating in learning rather than experiencing teaching. In such communities of practice, learning takes place through many modes including observation, demonstration and application, rather than through the passive transmission of knowledge. But most modern schools are not communities of practice because hierarchical relationships between teachers and learners place teachers in a uni-directional position of authority and power over pupils.

However, through whole school development schools can become communities of practice in which pupils are legitimate participants (Lave and Wenger, 1991), active citizens in a *process* of learning by doing (John, 1996). In communities of practice learning is contextually situated as knowledge is socially constructed through pupils' active participation in actions that are considered in and applied to local contexts. The consequence is that the outcomes of whole school approaches to EE/ESD may differ from one socio-environmental context to another. Learning is neither socially constructed nor simply a response to stimuli from the social or natural environment (see Figure 2.3). Learning is situated because it is both socio-culturally constructed and located in a community of practice that derives its legitimacy from its integration of local socio-cultural and environmental issues. The arrows in Figure 2.3 show the directions in which learning take place and knowledge is created.

Figure 2.3: Behaviourist, constructivist and situated learning (Based on Gough and Price, 2004)

Learning	Behaviourist	Constructivist/ cognitive	Situated/contextual
Motivation	External	Internal	Engaged participation
Knowledge	Corresponds to external social/ environmental realities	Socially constructed by a process of intersubjective agreement	Socially constructed within external social/ environmental contexts
	Human individual's understandings ↑ Environment/ society	Human individual's understandings ↓ Environment/ society	Human individual's understandings ↑↓ Environment/society

Some characteristics of whole school approaches

Besides integrating the five strands shown in Figure 2.1, whole school approaches have practical implications within each of these strands. The most important implication is the focus on process, on the social organisation of learning and the translation of this learning into action. This does not mean that outcomes are unimportant as Bowers' (1997) blueprint for a green campus shows:

- integrating environmental justice into all subjects
- improving ecological literacy (the understanding of biological conservation and the political basis of conserving societies)
- studying local equal opportunities issues
- conducting environmental audits
- developing ethically and environmentally friendly purchasing
- reducing waste
- maximising energy efficiency
- making sustainability a priority in land use, transport and building

Bowers clearly sees the need to link formal and non-formal curricula and descriptions of these outcomes are useful provided they are not prescriptions but suggestions requiring sensitive translation to new contexts (see Chapter Five). Prescriptions can impose an uncritical orthodoxy that conflicts with notions of EE/ESD as a situated process with the active participation of pupils and adults, collaborative school cultures and community links at its core. Bowers indicates that whole school development will not work without the knowledge imparted through the formal curriculum and that values such as justice need to be addressed in curriculum subjects. Based on their review of a number of national programmes designed to support whole school approaches, Henderson and Tilbury (2004) identify the characteristics of such approaches:

- participatory learning
- integration of the sustainability message across the formal curriculum
- leadership that places sustainability at the heart of school practice
- whole school participation
- regular CPD for teaching, support staff and other stakeholders
- greening of the school and its physical surroundings
- reducing the school's ecological footprint
- regular monitoring, reflection and evaluation

- practitioner research
- partnerships
- school culture and practices that reflect key messages from the formal curriculum

Active participation

Conventional ideologies of childhood render pupils passive because they fail to recognise the positive contribution that pupils can make to decision-making in schools (James and Prout, 1997). Pupils also interpret the world differently from adults, not because of any developmental deficiencies but because they grow up in a distinctive childhood culture. There is a growing desire among the young to be taken seriously, to influence their living conditions and improve their environment (Posch, 1996). For education to encourage active citizenship, childhood has to be seen as part of society with pupils as social agents (Rudduck and Flutter, 2000). Associating democratic education with whole school development would assist the expansion of pupil participation in schools because teachers, although sometimes cautious about democratic/participative education, generally support school development because it has become a mainstream movement.

If EE and ESD are to empower pupils and communities to live more sustainably by reducing their environmental impact on the planet, pupils have to participate in the discussion and selection of sustainable actions. Children's views must be taken seriously by facilitating their participation at the higher levels shown in Table 2.1. But while the high levels of participation shown on Table 2.1 offer the prospect of pupil empowerment, the table neglects community empowerment by omitting the joint initiation of ideas by children and adults. Thus whole school development necessitates a change from top-down curriculum planning to the active participation of pupils in negotiating the content and nature of their own learning within the environment in which this learning occurs. Although participation is endorsed in the UN Convention on the Rights of the Child (1989), the convention only requires adults to identify children's views: it does not require children to be involved in decision-making.

Participation is necessary because many young people do not feel that school helps them to understand issues of social and environmental justice or to be involved in local or global action (Holden, 1998). As young people get older they become more pessimistic about what they can do to make the planet a better place (Hicks and Holden, 1995). Although young people

Table 2.1: Ladder of participation (Based on Hart, 1997).

No.	Level	
1	Child initiated, shared decisions with adults	**Degrees of participation**
2	Child initiated and directed	
3	Adult initiated shared decisions with children	
4	Child consulted and informed	
5	Child assigned but informed	
6	Tokenism when children seem to have a voice but have little or no say in the choice of a subject or the means of communicating it	**Degrees of non-participation**
7	Decoration when children are involved by for example wearing T-shirts that demonstrate a cause that they know little or nothing about	
8	Manipulation when adults knowingly use children to convey adults' own views.	

generally have positive environmental attitudes they do not necessarily relate them to their own lives and material aspirations. And when they act: their actions are more related to energy conservation and recycling than to green consumerism (Rickinson, 2001).

In schools without a school council, few pupils believe that things could be different and that there are ways of learning to be a citizen in school (Davies, 1999). But where school councils exist they may socialise hypocrisy and dilute children's rights if they are limited to discussion of institutional practices such as catering and recycling. If this happens, schools councils degenerate into forums for damage limitation in which discussions of the formal curriculum or teaching are usually off-limits, rather than being venues for proactive decision-making (Holden, 1998).

School councils function best as part of a whole school democratic practice that is embedded at the classroom, school and community levels (Holden, 1998). Councils can extend pupil participation to all facets of Figure 2.1 by, for example:

- giving pupils influence over curriculum content and pedagogy
- interviewing prospective teachers
- mediating playground disputes
- conducting audits and becoming researchers
- evaluating their schools

■ deliberating and implementing institutional practices such as energy conservation

High level participation (Table 2.1) helps pupils to see that they can educate each other with less reliance on teachers and try to change those school structures that limit their agency (Rudduck and Flutter, 2000). Although pupils want to participate more in influencing school culture than changing the formal curriculum, when schools change by addressing values such as intellectual challenge and fairness, at the request of schools councils, pupils become more committed to learning (Rudduck and Flutter, 2000).

However, the notion of participation is problematic. In *The Council of Europe's Pupil Participation Project* pupils' notions of participation ranged from election to selection and included the need to educate their teachers about schools councils. This project revealed some unusual understandings of participation. Some pupils believed that the success of democratic classrooms lay in patient, tolerant teachers and obedient pupils (Council of Europe, 2000). But obedience is counterproductive if it rests on control achieved through ethical codes that schools impose rather than negotiate with their pupils. Pupils are not always comfortable with the changing roles that participation requires, especially as part of the participation agenda is to appreciate that some ideas may be impossible to implement. High achieving pupils in particular can have difficulty in adjusting to schools in which competition is not emphasised and rewarded. Such potential limitations may have to be addressed in a school if pupil participation is to thrive.

Democratic, collaborative school cultures

A whole school ethos besides promoting participation and community links should advocate a collaborative democratic culture of communication and decision-making based on mutual recognition and respect. Collaborative cultures (Nias *et al*, 1989) or active schools (Smyth and Hattam, 2002) are built on the belief that individuals and groups should be valued, because individuals are inseparable from groups and the best way of promoting the values of EE/ESD is through openness and a sense of mutual security. The development of collaborative or active cultures means that teachers' roles become less isolated and more associated with teams. Some of the factors which influence the culture of a school are its beliefs in childhood and how pupils should be treated, the headteacher's leadership style and management skills, school size, age range, background of children, physical setting, the community the school serves and resources (Littledyke, 1997). Collaborative cultures need to:

- be organised and efficient
- be proactive rather than reactive
- draw on theory
- have focused discussions about making decisions
- be based on written records (Fullan and Hargreaves, 1992)

If collaborative cultures are to develop, school staff need to be proficient in interpersonal skills and knowledgeable about group processes such as communication and conflict resolution (Pollard, 1985). In EE/ESD collaborative cultures also involve progressively stronger links between schools and their local communities for the seeds of sustainability lie in extending collaboration (Ridley, 1996).

As with participation not all forms of collaboration are without their problems. *Balkanisation* occurs when collaboration remains within but not between groups. This results in friction between subject-based groups or *cliques* in schools. The degree of collaboration within the culture of a school also looks different according to whose perspective is being taken. Culture and collaboration are not the property of any one group in a school: teachers, support staff, pupils or governors. School culture is continuously constructed by struggles within and between these groups (Smyth and Hattam, 2002). The links with parents may be the most important feature of collaborative cultures, because they form purposeful alliances outside schools that help to establish moral meaning and to disseminate the school's message (Fullan, 1999).

Democratic collaboration is about the common good, not just self-interest, so democratic schools are concerned with collaboration and cooperation rather than with competition (Beane and Apple, 1999). Pupils believe that democratic classrooms display tolerance, mutual respect, valuing of individuals, active participation, listening and fairness (Council of Europe, 2000). According to Aspin (1995) the principles of a democratic institution include: equality, freedom, tolerance, consideration of other people's interests and respect for other people. Experiencing these values through informal social networks and interactions that make participative decisions in schools is important because committees and meetings can symbolise a democracy that is representative rather than participative.

Collaboration does not mean a conformity that stifles disagreement because collaborative cultures foster a professionalism based on criticism and debate as school staff work in closer social spaces (Pollard, 1985). There is safety in these spaces to express the dissenting opinions that are rarely formally expressed in more authoritarian school cultures (Nias *et al*, 1989). Collaborative cultures promote:

- a strong sense of identity
- pragmatic problem-solving
- flexible leadership
- open communication
- the setting of goals congruent with the school's context (Pollard, 1985).

This collaborative whole school agenda places great responsibility on adults as moral agents. In whole school approaches to EE/ESD schools and adults model sustainability not by being the custodians of the correct values but by acting as consistently as possible with the values they uphold. Role models who are consistent in their judgments of moral predicaments generally have greater impact on children's moral reasoning than those who disagree with each other (Bandura, 1986). This discussion and articulation of values is crucial: it is unethical to indoctrinate pupils into values held by adults or to avoid discussing values with children because this creates the impression that the development of society is established and beyond children's influence (Mogensen, 1995). In this context the non-formal curriculum is arguably a more important arena for values education than the formal curriculum.

> The child is a witness; the child is an ever attentive witness of grown-up morality – or lack thereof; the child looks and looks for cues as to how one ought to behave, and finds them galore as we parents and teachers go about our lives, making choices, addressing people, showing in action our rock-bottom assumptions, desires and values, and thereby telling those young observers much more than we may realise. (Coles, 1997: 5)

Education is a relational activity between human beings. Where positive relationships are established they can open the door to high self-esteem and the determination of pupils to please not only adults but also themselves (Coles, 1997). Such relationships are not built solely on adults' intellectual capacities. They are also deeply rooted in their body language and the subliminal messages conveyed through the non-formal curriculum.

Formal curriculum, critical pedagogy and institutional practice
Although it seems inappropriate to specify curriculum content in EE/ESD as the formal curriculum and institutional practices should privilege process while content is locally decided, some approaches can be suggested. Given

43

the complexity of the environmental crisis and sustainable development, it is essential that EE/ESD promote more holistic, cross-curricular approaches to understanding and problem solving (Greig *et al*, 1989). However, these approaches need not be limited to interdisciplinarity, approaches that address the interconnections in knowledge through learning by doing. Holistic approaches can emerge from a subject-based formal curriculum if these operate within a coherent whole school approach in which cross-curricular connections are made through the participative processes that link a formal and non-formal curriculum, in part by addressing local issues. For example holistic education could draw heavily on systemic thinking (WWF, 2005). Using a technique such as life cycle analysis is one way of analysing food products to identify sustainable solutions, such as healthy eating and local sourcing of food that can be adopted in a school's catering. Here curriculum knowledge and understanding are integrated with learning to act as active citizens.

Critical pedagogy (Giroux, 1996) is also crucial to situated learning in EE/ESD because it questions existing lifestyles so that more environmentally just and equitable alternatives can be considered. By deconstructing subject boundaries and creating new spaces in which knowledge can be integrated and reproduced, it enables learning to take place and reveals where power is located in society. The stereotypes, prejudices and simplifications on which so much social and ecological injustice breeds need to be challenged in schools. But critical pedagogy is not the only practice that contributes to environmentally sustainable lifestyles. Futures education is important because it develops the ability to identify those cultural patterns with the potential to contribute to future sustainable lifestyles (Hicks, 2001).

The essence of institutional practice in whole school approaches is its coherence in putting into practice the knowledge and values acquired in the formal curriculum. Technical/economic outcomes should focus on reducing the environmental impact of the school and its community by conserving resources, reducing waste, promoting healthy living, and designing and managing indoor and outdoor spaces in an aesthetically pleasing and ecologically friendly way. Fortunately, institutional practice and community links are the least centrally controlled and inspected aspects of schools provision, which makes it easier to initiate whole school approaches in these areas as the Maltese case study (Chapter Nine) shows.

Whole school approaches also have implications for evaluation and assessment because both are necessary for critical review. Assessment should promote cooperation rather than competition by being developmental i.e. longitudinal and personal rather than comparative i.e. latitudinal and inter-personal and review should clearly privilege an element of self-evaluation (see Chapter Three). Educational practices should not only be judged by the skills and knowledge they impart now but by how they promote the self-efficacy that pupils need in the future (Bandura, 1986).

Conclusion: what is the evidence for whole school approaches?
Community links are best developed alongside a sense of community within school. The small school movement regards the quality of a community as a function of its size. Research in the USA shows that the evidence for small schools is compelling. Small schools have:

- better attendance rates
- higher test scores
- greater participation in after-school activities
- lower truancy rates
- less substance abuse and gang membership
- more pupils with positive attitudes to school
- closer bonds between peers and teachers
- more involved parents
- teachers who are more innovative (Tasker, 2001)

Although the case for large schools is largely economic, the higher economic costs of small schools can be nullified by the social costs to society of high drop-out rates in large schools (Tasker, 2001). This does not mean that com-munity quality is exclusive to small schools: it can be created in large schools by establishing smaller social units that give pupils some of the cultural benefits of smaller schools.

There is also evidence more specifically for whole school approaches to EE/ESD Rauch (2000). These can lead to:

- reductions in vandalism
- increased waste separation
- energy saving
- marked reductions in aggression and destruction
- more fervent student participation for example when students painted classrooms and planted trees in their school grounds to *their own designs* (Rauch, 2000)

Farrer with Hawkes (2000) confirm that whole school development has a positive effect on playground behaviour. By thinking, investigating and writing about their community, pupils reconfirm their own and their family's worth and gain knowledge about the problems that they and society as a whole must confront (Peterson, 1999). Breiting and Mogensen (1999) found that almost 75 per cent of a sample of Danish pupils considered that concrete actions to solve environmental problems should be an integral part of education.

In summary, whole school approaches are concerned with pupils' overall achievement. Children acquire skills and knowledge more easily if they interact with more knowledgeable adults in a whole school context (Holden and Clough, 1998) in which they develop a strong sense of morality (Coles, 1997) because they act out values in an emotional secure culture in which they are likely to achieve but can occasionally fail in safety.

The vision of whole school approaches presented here is not a blueprint. While each school will develop its own vision of development, these visions will change in the process. Visions change because external circumstances change. For example the recent revelation from Germany that spending money on energy conservation in buildings is more cost effective than generating electricity from wind power may influence schools to invest more money in energy conservation measures rather than in green energy providers. But visions will also change because collaborative school cultures and active pupil and community participation encourage debate and the discussion of ideas.

Schools should not try to reach a fully integrated whole school approach (see Figure 2.1) from scratch but should select the priorities that suit their local context and are achievable. Setting up a school council or a recycling scheme is much more achievable than trying to generate green energy in the school grounds. As whole school development proceeds, schools need to ask themselves what their next step should be in forging stronger links between the five strands shown in Figure 2.1. The case studies in Chapters Six to Ten show schools at different stages of developing whole school approaches. None of these schools will achieve perfect integration between the five strands. But whatever the outcome, the schools must recognise that these are achieved through democratic, participatory processes that foster and support active, collaborative school cultures. It is the journey, the processes by which we educate children, that matters more than the outcomes or the destination.

3

Reflective living practice: analytical case studies and school development

Arjen E.J. Wals

Introduction

In this book EE and ESD[4] are viewed as participatory processes contributing to both school development and the creation of a more sustainable community. The emphasis is on creating space for innovation and improving the relationships between people and between people and their community environment. EE/ESD is seen as contributing to the development of autonomous thinking about issues that affect the quality of human life and of that of other species. An emphasis on autonomous thinking about sustainability issues suggests that it would be inappropriate to prescribe behavioural outcomes that a learning activity or sequence of activities needs to foster (Jickling, 1992; Sauvé, 1996). After all, it would be highly questionable to prescribe a particular set of desired behaviours when the idea of sustainable development is surrounded with so much uncertainty and controversy, is value-laden, has so many different meanings, and is so dependent upon local conditions. It is more educational to engage people actively and critically, young and old, in searching for meaning, exploring options and finding their own pathways towards sustainable living, than to lead them into prescribed outcomes.

In this chapter the idea of reflective living practice is introduced as a concept that can helps schools design their own pathways towards school development and sustainability. This reflective living practice is considered an integral part of school development that is internally driven by the members of the school community. It can be documented in critical case studies, which can not only both understand and transform the reality of a school, but can also stimulate similar learning in other contexts. This concept of the critical transfer of learning, rather then uncritical borrowing is located in the notion of situated learning in which learning is not simply socially constructed but is created by intersubjective agreement between people in specific cultural and environmental contexts (see Figure 2.3). The idea of reflective living practice and the use of critical case studies can help schools in simultaneously improving the quality of the learning environment and in strengthening a school's contribution to a more sustainable community.

I will first embed the use of critical case studies for whole school development in the tradition of action research and in the context of community problem-solving (Stapp, *et al*, 1996). Self-evaluation is introduced as a tool for understanding and reviewing one's own practice and a necessary component of the development of critical case studies. The differences between cases/case records, celebratory case stories and critical case studies and the essential elements that critically analytical case study needs to include will be explored. A heuristic or set of guiding questions and signposts for critically analytical case studies that are helpful for members of a school community in reflecting on their own practice, but also in documenting and sharing this practice with others, can be found in Chapter Five. This heuristic has been used as a guide in generating the abstracts for the case studies of the five European schools presented in Chapters Six to Ten.

A critique of evaluation as measurement

Evaluation is often confused with measurement. Schools are increasingly under pressure to show hard evidence that their pupils are making progress. In several core subject areas such as reading, mathematics and science, testing agencies are continuously working to develop better tests for measuring pupil performance. As a result, much of the learning in schools is driven by tests that privilege learning outcomes which can be measured by a test over those that are less easily measured. Some groups within the EE research community have responded by developing equally sophisticated tests to assess concepts such as environmental literacy or pupil empowerment. Tests are often standardised so that groups of pupils can be compared – for example the environmental literacy rates of inner-city children compared with those of rural children – and these groups can even be ranked and categorised.

In EE/ESD the focus is often not on measurable learning goals and universal questions and answers that can be found irrespective of where we live. Instead the focus is on learning goals which are not so easily measured but are significant in requiring a deep learning process affecting the whole human being. The more meaningful a learning activity is, the harder it is to measure its outcomes by a simple test.

Human ideas, experiences, and intentions are not objective things like molecules and atoms. Nevertheless, like their colleagues in the natural sciences, many educational researchers attempt to use objective evaluation methods that allow for control, predictability and the ability to generalise. Knowledge and human interests are interwoven and this is reflected in the choice of evaluative methods and the ends to which such methods are put. Unless the ends served by our evaluation are examined, there is a risk that prediction and control may exclude other ends such as improved understanding among people, the release of human potential and the development of a sustainable relationship with our surroundings.

It is very tempting to structure the content matter of EE/ESD and the way it is presented to pupils by using hierarchical, universal goals and objectives through which outside experts determine:

- what pupils need to learn in terms of knowledge, attitudes, values and skills
- a curriculum design that consists of measurable/quantifiable goals and objectives
- how to implement the programme
- how to test to what extent the goals and objectives are realised
- how to modify the programme and re-instruct the teacher (see Figure 3.1)

In the worst-case scenario, pupils become a data source (Fielding, 2001) and the teachers an implementation instrument. This widely used positivistic approach to educational innovation often results in ignoring the pupils' own ideas and experiences and the classroom experience and expertise of the teacher. Teachers and pupils are not seen as being capable of determining the content of their own education nor of setting their own goals and objectives. Nor are they allowed to evaluate their own teaching and learning. Alienation between testing agencies and the school community, and disempowerment of teachers and pupils who have been denied a role in shaping and evaluating their own education, is a frequent result of this top-down approach. Unfortunately, the measured curriculum is still spreading, even though its negative side effects on school development and human development have been well documented (Kohn, 2000).

I believe there is a way of evaluating that is compatible with the ideas presented in Chapters One and Two, provided that evaluation is not viewed just as a data collecting activity for ranking purposes but rather as a process that seeks to understand and improve the school and its community through simultaneous action and reflection with all the parties involved. To do this emphasis must be placed on:

- documenting and describing human experience and intentions
- using a range of diagnostic instruments
- using the observations of the teachers, pupils, school management, school support staff and parents
- interpreting results with all the participants
- relating the results to the foundations, goals, direction and objectives of whole school development as agreed upon by the school community
- discussing ways to adjust the curriculum, classroom practice and school management as a result of newly obtained insights

In this perspective on evaluation there should be a pedagogical end in that the evaluation itself has educational value. This view of internally driven (self-motivated) and contextual (embedded in the specific situation of one school) self-evaluation will have to co-exist with the other forms or evaluation or assessment often prescribed by educational authorities. However, the balance between the two may vary greatly from school to school, from one cultural context to another and from nation to nation.

There are two extremes in the evaluation continuum. The first is a top-down or vertical approach, primarily driven by authorities outside the school community to ensure that every school meets certain standards or minimum requirements (see the left hand column of Figure 3.1). Evaluation schemes, tools and instruments are developed and tested by outside experts and made available for all schools. The resulting standardised evaluation schemes claim to help educational authorities to identify the strengths and weaknesses of every school and to compare schools. These vertical evaluation schemes can help experts and inspectors to diagnose potential problems and prescribe solutions.

The second extreme is a bottom-up or horizontal approach (see the right hand side of Figure 3.1) that is primarily driven from within the school by the

Figure 3.1: A comparison of top-down and bottom-up evaluation (Based on Pace, 1996a)

Action research and community problem-solving

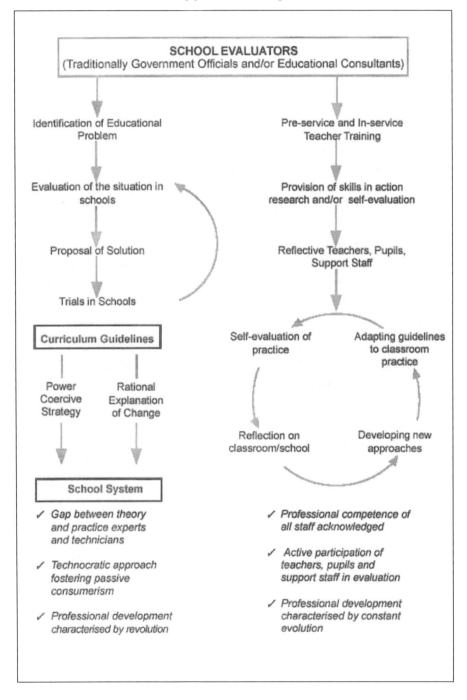

needs of students, teachers, administrators and parents. This approach stresses continuous action and reflection and regular reviews of goals and objectives and the methods used to achieve them. The success of this participatory strategy depends on people's ability and willingness to consider change, to be introspective, to be expressive, to be open towards criticism and self-criticism and to be sensitive to the ideas of other members of the school community. In the next section the bottom-up approach towards evaluation is taken further by introducing the idea of self-evaluation within an action research and community problem-solving framework.

The introduction to this chapter presents a view of education and school development involving participation, self-determination, autonomy and critical reflection. This view of education uses evaluation methods which do not distort communication by manipulating and controlling school and teachers. Evaluation methods should allow those who are most affected by education and educational change to express their ideas to identify the changes they find necessary. If a school wants to realise educational change then it is crucial that all actors involved jointly assess and define the school's situation, how it was arrived at, the imagined outcome of the educational change process and the way to transform the present situation into a more desirable one (Elliott, 1991, 1993; Wals, 1993; Hart, 1997).

This view of school-based development, implementation and evaluation differs from the more traditional view of educational change, which maintains that outside experts can best diagnose schools and develop prescriptions for changes they consider necessary. In situations where teachers, administrators, pupils and parents feel they are rarely consulted, the model of expert-based innovation seems inappropriate. Given the importance of involving the whole school community in the development, implementation and evaluation of educational change or an educational innovation, an action-research approach towards whole school development and sustainable living seems more appropriate (Wals *et al*, 1990; OECD, 1994; OECD-CERI, 1995).

Action research is both a methodology and a way of thinking. Sociologist Kurt Lewin (1946) is generally considered to be the founding father of this approach. Action research can be described as:

> ...a form of self-reflective inquiry undertaken by participants in social (including educational) situations in order to improve the rationality and justice of their own social or educational practices, their understanding of these practices and the situations in which the practices are carried out. (Kemmis, 1986: 42)

Action research requires the blending of theory and practice so that those who will be most affected by any proposed changes will help to decide what theories and experiences are the most meaningful and relevant. The blending of theory and practise requires praxis, a spirally developing concurrent process of evaluation, reflection and action (Lewin, 1946; Carr and Kemmis, 1986). While participants are engaged in a problem-solving process, they are continuously reflecting on their work and its effectiveness (Stapp *et al*, 1996). This is an active process: participants seek out the information they need, define their own problems and develop and try a range of solutions.

Community problem-solving provides a framework for employing action research in moving towards more sustainable communities. Lewin's methodology, adapted to schools, revolves around identifying and acting upon a local or school-based issue in cooperation with pupils and other affected people. Important elements of community problem-solving are:

- recognising a problem
- collecting, organising, and analysing information
- defining the problem from a variety of perspectives
- identifying, considering, and selecting alternative actions to take
- developing and carrying out a plan of action
- evaluating the outcome and the entire process (see Figure 3.2)

The inner spiral or second phase of the action research community problem-solving cycle follows the first phase shown on Figure 3.2. Second phases usually trigger successive and continuing cycles. In all these steps the human and material resources in the community are utilised whenever possible. The synthesis of action research and community problem-solving creates an inquiry process that enables teachers, pupils and other relevant groups to participate more fully in the planning, implementing and evaluating of educational activities, which are aimed at resolving an issue that the learners have identified for themselves (Stapp *et al*, 1996). An issue arises from the perceptions and experiences of the learners and the context in which education takes place. Throughout this action research community problem-solving process members of the school community ideally come to interpret their situation as requiring intervention, especially their own.

Self-evaluation
Self-evaluation is an integral part of action research and community problem-solving. It provides an opportunity for simultaneous action and reflection. When organised democratically, it can assist all members of the

Figure 3.2: The action research community problem-solving cycle

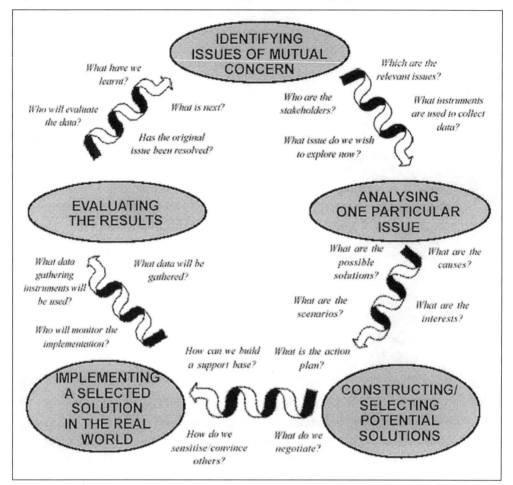

school community to identify where they are, the direction they would like to take and ways that might help them get there. Self-evaluation is about evaluating the quality of learning and the school environment from the perspective of the whole school community. It is a dynamic process that stresses the value of everyone's input: the child, the teacher, the parent, the institution and the community. But self-evaluation is also about improving practice and outcomes and not about judging, labelling and comparing. Self-evaluation is a process that keeps groups and individuals on track towards a self-determined goal but it clearly involves outcomes. It is feedback oriented and non-threatening. Figure 3.3 is an approach to describing styles of self-evaluation based on the degree of openness or closure of outcomes and the degree of hierarchy or participation in its processes. This model may be a useful one to use in assessing the nature of self-evaluation in your own school. In the context of whole school approaches, self-evaluation is defined as follows:

> Self-evaluation is an internally driven and empowering, semi-structured, systematic evaluation process involving all members of the school community in improving school practices which help contribute towards more sustainable futures. (SEEPS, 2004 (see Chapter 11))

Self-evaluation provides pupils with the opportunity to stop and review a particular situation. This enables the child to assimilate and internalise experience. It is mainly through this process that the child learns and grows from his/her experiences. A variety of tools is available for self-evaluation purposes, depending on the age of the child. Methods promoting self-ex-

Figure 3.3: Processes and outcomes in self-evaluation (Based on Wals and Jickling, 2002)

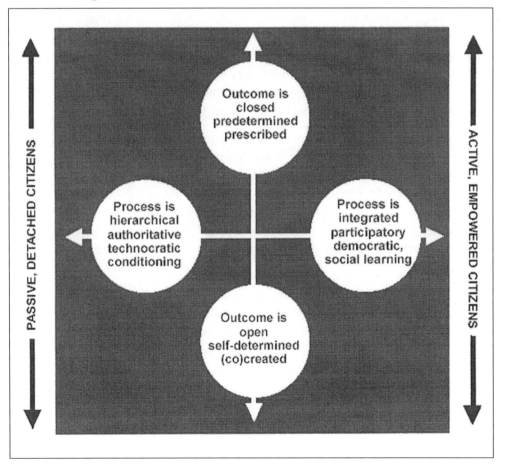

pression are particularly useful as they provide pupils with the freedom to express their own ideas in a way or language directly relevant to their experience, thus providing teachers with deeper insights into their pupils.

Self-evaluation provides teachers with the opportunity to reflect on the extent to which they are meeting the objectives set by a programme or by the teachers themselves. Self-evaluation can help in assisting teachers in the design of more effective lessons/programmes. Depending on the type of tool used, self-evaluation may help teachers to reflect on their attitudes, values and lifestyles, thus supporting professional development. Self-evaluation may also provide opportunities to review the effectiveness of policies and their impact on the different individuals within the school/community.

Good practice, best practice or just practice?

Case studies are often confused with stories of best practice or good practice. Although there may be a place for celebratory, feel good case studies in creating better schools, they can have serious negative side effects. The study may be rejected because it is biased in that successes and positive outcomes are privileged over negative ones, resulting in an inaccurate representation of what happened. And reading a celebratory case study can be depressing for teachers in less successful schools because it emphasises the failings of their own situation, making the best practice case study seem like a Utopian dream.

Feel good case studies can, in some instances, be inspiring and show possibilities not seen before, but this depends on how the case is written up. If the aim of the case study is to show others how good we are, rather than to inspire others by providing critical insights into how their practice might change, then it becomes a public relations tool which may be instrumental in achieving strategic objectives, but without much educational benefit to others.

Another shortcoming of many best practice case studies is that they tend to present practice as an attractive product emphasising design, presentation and tangible outcomes such as improved test scores, amount of energy conserved and waste reduced, while neglecting the process itself. Often the educational value of a case study does not lie in these products but in the critical insights into the processes underlying them. These processes take place in a rich context of complexity, uncertainty, risk, struggles, relationships, barriers and incentives. Some insight into both the processes and the context can help others in mirroring (Cassel and Giddens, 1993), reflecting on their ideas, the insights, experiences of others and their own practice in relation to the case study. The subtleties, nuances, and seemingly small facts left out of success stories often speak to crucial issues in fostering simultaneous school development and sustainability. Hence critically analytical case studies pay attention to detail and provide rich descriptions of continuously evolving practice in a way that invites the reader to relate the case to his/her own practice.

The quality of the dialectic that emerges when confronting the practice embodied in a case study with the reader's own practice shapes the pedagogical transfer value of a case study. Pedagogical transfer value refers to the potential of a particular case study to promote innovation beyond the context of the case itself. A good case study actively engages the reader with the text resulting in the mirroring of his/her experiences by reflecting on his/her ideas, insights, experiences and feelings relative to those of others and to those in the case study. In this process, attitudes and actions are likely to change. This mirroring may lead the learner to rethink ideas in the light of alternative, possibly contesting, viewpoints or ways of thinking about school development and creating a more sustainable community of learners.

In order to develop cases that are critical, highly reflective and have transformative qualities, we have used a heuristic for case study development. This heuristic basically consists of a set of guiding questions that can be used to build a case study but can also be used as a tool for self-evaluation (see Table 5.1).

Stepping stones for developing critical analytical case studies
How do we move from impressionistic feel good case studies towards case studies that have educative value in that they stimulate learning? How can case studies become more critical and reflective of practice at one's own school and at the same time be of interest to practitioners elsewhere? How can we strike some kind of balance between the call for universal models and prescriptions and the need for contextual relevance and meaning? Some critical guiding questions are helpful in this transition towards more critical and analytical case studies which can contribute to whole school improvement and sustainable development. The stepping stones and questions presented in Chapter Five build upon the work of Walker *et al*, (2004), which looked at case study research in this way.

In developing the framework of guiding questions for critical case study development, four broad areas are important (Walker *et al*, 2004). The first is

57

purpose. There should be a clear purpose for the case study and the study should address this purpose. Case studies are used in the Sustainability Education in European Primary Schools (SEEPS) project (Shallcross, 2004) (see Chapter Eleven) to document both the process and results of a school's attempts to integrate sustainable development or elements of it into the school curriculum or the school as an institution with its own ecological footprint. A particular interest in the SEEPS project is the link between school-based sustainable development and whole school development (see Chapter One). An exploration of the relationship between sustainable development and high quality learning environments is the overarching theme of the project. A more general goal of the case studies is to improve individual practice and that of others.

The second area is the roles of the players. It is important that all members of the school community who represent potentially diverging interests and values have a role in the case study. Their roles and the way their perspectives are utilised or reconciled needs to be addressed. If possible, the power base of players and institutions needs to be explored in a critically analytical case study: whose interests and goals are served by the innovation?

The third area concerns tensions between the universal and contextual. Every school is different and the ways in which sustainable development issues are dealt with in one school are deeply rooted in its particular reality. Therefore, it is important for a study to address how learning from one school can transform beyond its context. Lessons learned from a critically analytical case study are only transferable to other settings when generalising is viewed as a process of interaction between the reader and the author/s of the case study. This process requires the reader to relate the findings of a study to his or her own experiences. At the same time it requires the author to present the findings as subject to interpretation, adaptation and rejection (Wals and Alblas, 1997).

This approach differs from the more prescriptive 'what research says' approach. What educators learn about one school's experience in integrating sustainable development and education can raise consciousness of similar phenomena or issues that might be found in other schools (Eisner, 1991). Critical case studies of school innovation cannot claim that all schools will share similar issues or pathways of development. Instead these critical case studies present possibilities other schools might want to consider for transforming themselves. In a sense, generalising or transferring to another context is up to the reader. Elsewhere this has been referred to as case-inspired self-generalisation (Wals and Alblas, 1997). Critically analytical case studies differ in this way from celebratory case studies which often conclude with a checklist or set of recommendations.

The fourth area, mentioned by Walker *et al* (2004), is challenge. Whole school improvement and the creation of sustainable communities have both personal and shared elements. The inevitable social interaction that takes place in a community problem-solving process allows one to relate one's ideas, insights, experiences and feelings to those of others. In this process of mirroring (Cassel and Giddens, 1993), change takes place. This mirroring can be seen as challenging the ways of thinking involved in an institutional change process. It may create the dissonance needed to trigger the rethinking of ideas in light of alternative, possibly contesting, viewpoints or ways of thinking and feeling. At the same time experiences shared with others are likely to gain in importance. This is not to say that personal experiences which are kept private are insignificant. But shared viewpoints in collaborative cultures or ways of thinking and feeling give the learner a sense of competence and belonging to the community of learners and practice (Lave and Wenger, 1991). A challenge for the writer of a critical case study is to write it in such a way that it challenges the reader to relate personal experiences to the experiences in the case study.

Robinson (1993) outlines a set of key questions asked in this critical case study form of action research:

- What is the problem or issue?
- How have practitioners attempted to solve the problem? (What is their theory of action, the constraints, strategies and consequences of their actions?)
- How is the solution judged to be adequate?
- How do we build a more adequate theory?

These questions are best addressed by a community of learners representing a variety of perspectives on the issue in question in a cyclical process of simultaneous action and reflection during which theory and practice are integrated (Wals and Alblas, 1997). The set of considerations (Table 5.1) are based on the work of Walker *et al*, (2004) and form the basis for the critical case study methodology used in the case studies documented in Chapters Six to Ten. The questions in the guidelines shown in Table 5.1 are not intended to be a prescriptive checklist but a list of suggested enquiries that schools and teachers can modify.

Conclusion

This chapter has presented an argument for improving school self-conscious critique or reflexivity by employing evaluation strategies that promote participation, self-determination, empowerment and collaborative learning. The action research and community problem-solving approach introduced in this chapter (Figure 3.2) represents a number of concrete steps and actions that members of the school community can use. They can be used to create a more sustainable school in terms of the learning environment it creates and the role it plays in sustaining the community it supports and by which it is supported. The idea of critical case studies is to learn from reflexive practice. Using a range of questions, organised in some basic evaluation categories, the drivers, processes, outcomes and impacts of school-based innovation can be followed, evaluated, documented and shared with others through a range of networks.

However, the road to reflexive educational practice is long and taxing. The ideas and principles underlying such practice may appear sound and sensible, but creating a school climate conducive to reflexivity and the development of the necessary competences among school administrators, teachers and pupils, to be able to reflect, critique, mirror, listen and respond to lessons learnt, poses tremendous challenges. The case studies presented in Chapters Six to Ten illustrate the need, possibilities and challenges for developing a culture of reflective living practice in schools. None of these are exactly like the vision presented in this chapter. In fact, some illustrate how hard it is to move away from traditional external expert driven evaluations. But they represent a first step and do show that the challenge of sustainable development can be a catalyst for moving towards more participatory and reflective school communities that recognise more fully the tremendous potential for change.

4

Change, action and school-focused professional development

Tony Shallcross

Introduction

Change is seldom linear and well-ordered,
progressing smoothly from one situation to another.
Change is not always the same as progress,
with each stage a logical development of the one before.
Change does not automatically confer improvements,
even though this is its intention.
Change induces tension and anxiety,
but generates excitement and exhilaration.
Change is frustrating and exhausting,
but also a spur to greater things.
But without change, life is boring.
(Rodway, in Shallcross, 2004).

Implementing and leading change (Goleman, 1998) are emotional as well as rational processes (Robinson and Shallcross, 1998). Although change is a process, outcomes are not ignored. The nature of change is inextricably linked with results. Change is also unpredictable because it produces emergent, unexpected features that arise from the social interactions within complex systems that produce change (Sterling, 2001). These emergent features are central properties of complexity and important in educational change. Change is an unpredictable process that involves action, cognition and emotion. However, there are at least two problems that arise when educational change is discussed. First, the failure to recognise the special nature of schools as organisations whose primary business is learning, not profit, and second the relatively limited research into the organisational features of school life (Ball, 1987).

School development promotes whole school approaches and school self-evaluation. Whether these processes are driven from within or outside schools, they are contingent upon the professional development of teachers (Evans, 1993). Professional development is crucial in the management and leadership of change for school development. In the organisation of such professional development, distinguishing between rationale (why), vision (what), design (how) and evaluation are important if school development is to be successful. In discussing how change can be managed and led in schools and why school-focused professional development is arguably the most appropriate strategy for promoting whole school development, this chapter will draw significantly on the writing of Michael Fullan.

Change
Education as school effectiveness

The late twentieth century saw increased centralised control of education in many European educational systems. Greater use of coercive, power-over strategies of management (Begg, 2000) usually accompanied this centralisation. This centralisation saw an associated decrease in the professional power of teachers, especially over the formal curriculum. This point is illustrated in at least three of the case studies in this book (Chapters Six, Eight and Nine). This effectiveness approach to educational change is based on the management of performance as the main route to school improvement (see Chapter One). Effectiveness is usually judged against standards or targets that are externally assessed and verified. This is a paradigm of change in which standards have become confused with standardisation, maxim with mandate (Shulman, 1987), achievement with attainment and effectiveness with improvement.

The school effectiveness paradigm often operates through a tyranny of numbers (Boyle, 2001) in which only that which is quantifiable can be assessed and only that which can be assessed can change. Progress equates with achieving ever increasing targets, such as a higher position in a league table based on a higher percentage of pupils achieving higher test results. To achieve these better test results, education frequently becomes more didactic and the parameters that identify acceptable change are usually imposed from outside and/or above, especially through inspections or assessments. But even within this paradigm educators may have more power than they assume. Those who work in the welfare state, including school staff, have the greatest potential for forging links between power-over and power-to dynamics of change (Begg, 2000). With the appropriate professional development, those workers who have to contend with hierarchically imposed change, while they simultaneously work to empower patients or pupils can develop the potential to promote transformatory change.

There are some significant exceptions to this effectiveness, performance based approach in Europe, perhaps most notably in the Finnish educational system. The case study in Chapter Seven gives some insights into the more organic and developmental approach to education and evaluation adopted in Finland. It is interesting and revealing to note how well Finnish pupils perform in international tests of attainment such as the OECD PISA (Programme for International Student Assessment) studies. This level of performance may represent fledgling evidence for a causal link between pupil achievement and high levels of pupil attainment when achievement rather than attainment is prioritised. The other case studies also show, to varying degrees, how individual schools can be successful in promoting whole school development even when the larger educational system may be more attuned to school effectiveness approaches to educational change.

Power and the nature of change

The most important thing to recognise about change, especially in relation to whole school development, is that it is a process/journey rather than an outcome/destination. The processes by which change occurs may often be more important than its outcomes, especially in EE and ESD[5]. Enthusiasts for EE/ESD and/or whole schools development are often driven by powerful visions of outcomes based on morally compelling rationales. These visions and rationales may lead enthusiasts to get carried away and consequently not recognise that others perceive change differently. This is certainly true in EE/ESD where addressing issues such as poverty and environmental degradation are often driven by strong ethical motives. For many environmental philosophers (Naess, 1995b; Oelschlaeger, 1995; O'Sullivan, 1999) redressing these inequities requires a radical intellectual transformation that develops rationales and visions based on wider, more ecologically based concepts of community (see Chapter Two).

If such ethically-driven environmental visions are combined with educational visions of whole school approaches (see Figure 2.1) these images can cause anxiety, fear or even hostility for some school staff because these visions will appear difficult, if not impossible, to achieve. What worries teachers is not necessarily the merit of an alternative vision or rationale but the arduous nature of the journey needed to transform schools, in this case from currently unsustainable, largely curriculum-driven agendas, into more holistic, sustainable practices. It is the design of change, especially when this entails giant leaps forward, that appears problematic, rather then the integrity of visions of whole school development.

Change becomes even more unsettling when those with power over schools impose it on teachers who have little or no control over the processes of change. Notions of participatory democracy and collaboration, which are central to whole school development, are based much more in grassroots notions of power-to schools, pupils and communities rather than top-down, power-over school communities (Begg, 2000). This is not to argue that any situation in which change occurs is either one or other of these power relationships, most situations will combine both in some proportion. But because power-to schools is likely to engender feelings of collective agency and self-efficacy it is much more likely to be acceptable and productive in engendering deep-seated change (Begg, 2000). For such deep-seated change to occur it is important that schools *feel* that they have some control over their own destinies:

> When ministries, management and research agencies outside the school system give schools real tasks to do and actually use the data generated by schools, the instruction takes on additional meaning for the pupils. They learn that their input and effort and concern are important for society. They can make a difference. (Benedict, 1999: 445)

Often what top-down, power-over approaches to educational change produce is reorientation (McLaughlin, 1991) or superficial change (Blenkin *et al*, 1992) that absorbs the language of change but not its substance. Sterling (2001) distinguishes between two types of reorientation change: accommodatory that adapts to the existing dominant educational values or reformatory change that is critically reflective of the process of change but not of the social, ecological or educational values that underpin it (see Table 5.7). Whole school development in EE/ESD is more concerned with substantive or transformatory change that involves a fundamental rethinking of the meaning of schooling, the deeper structures of the curriculum and the school as an institution and the ultimate values on which these are based (see Table 4.3).

Although too much premature vision of outcomes can be blinding and potentially disempowering for some school staff (Fullan, 1999), for reasons outlined in Chapter Two, vision should not be relegated from discussions about the initiation of change (see Chapter One). Although vision is a feature that normally comes later in the process of change (Fullan and Hargreaves, 1992) process-based visions are important in the promotion of educational change:

> If there is one justifiable vision that is generic to our argument, it is a vision of particular ways of working together and of commitment to perpetual learning and improvement .... process visions about how schools work together are central to continuing improvement. (Fullan and Hargreaves, 1992: 122)

The same argument can also be applied to visions of EE/ESD. For some, authentic EE is rooted in experience of the world outside school (Uzzell *et al*, 1994; Elliot, 1999). But there are dangers in setting community links as the *sine qua non* of all EE programmes: this may lead schools to get involved in over-ambitious projects which lead to debilitating stultification rather than facilitating progress. While the view of schools being linked to their local community represents one of the most effective ways that pupils can have influence as global citizens, such spatial prescriptions partly miss the point. Community involvement should not be regarded as the essence of EE/ESD, but as one of many possible coordinates on a quest in which the journey is more important than the destination. A school with a highly developed internally focused, participatory culture could be considered to have more developed EE/ESD than a school with high levels of community linkage achieved through imposed collaboration and participation (see Table 2.1).

Change in schools results from the influence of both social structures and personal agency but structure and agency are inter-related (Giddens, 1979) and linked to notions of power. Power in the interrelational sense '.... concerns the capability of actors to secure outcomes where the realisation of these outcomes depends upon the agency of others' (Giddens, 1979: 93). Power underpins the capacity for change, a capacity that is traditionally expressed in people's success in persuading others to see things from their perspective. So changing any facet of a school or its local environment is best achieved with the support of many groups of people: teachers, support staff, pupils, parents and other stakeholders, as reflected in all the case studies. These groups need to collaborate as agents of change to achieve the school development that leads to sustainable social and environmental change. The social structures and power dynamics through which these groups interrelate can radically alter their capacity and/or willingness to achieve change.

Change and moral purpose

Whole school development in EE/ESD is an endeavour fused with moral purpose; it is not just about identifying the correct moral actions, it is about mobilising moral commitment (Fullan, 1999). Moral purpose cannot be achieved solely through externally driven agendas as it necessitates empathy and relationships that develop through contacts between diverse social groups. For change to be sustainable, moral purpose needs to be combined with the practical wisdom that is reflected in successful designs for change. Moral purpose permits selection of the right ends, while practical wisdom allows selection of the right means (Blenkin *et al*, 1992). Because moral purpose is complex (Fullan, 1999), it means that school communities need to debate ideas about power and purpose. These debates are fundamental to the participative, democratic approach associated with whole school development. Thus change that translates moral purpose into sustainable actions is not only a philosophical task but also a complex cultural, psychological and practical endeavour. This link between moral purpose and complexity is best explained by Goerner's (cited in Fullan, 1999) observations about dynamic evolution:

- changing minds is a lot more efficient than changing bodies
- learning is best done in collaborative groups provided that these groups share a moral commitment to the greater good
- the challenge of dealing with the intricacy of change is to keep smallness under an ever growing umbrella of connections

Not learning these essentially social lessons is the reason why so much organisational change fails. Many organisations focus on changing the economic aspects of production and forget that their true purpose is to perform as social enterprises laden with moral purpose (Argyris and Schön, 1996).

Change, self-regulation and interrelationalism

Recent developments in chaos theory support the process-focused approach to change by adding the notion of self-making, self-regulating systems that make order possible (Capra, 1996). Self-regulation is very important in whole school development in EE/ESD because it links both ecological and social theories (Giddens, 1979) and is consequently fundamental to an integrated perception of transformative educational and environmental change. In educational contexts this conception of change is concerned with design and aspiration rather than planning and targets. Design and aspiration are open, organic, participative and iterative while planning and targeting are specific, mechanistic, controlling and time bound (Sterling, 2001). In self-regulating systems change requires a trust in the processes of collaborative learning that may be incomplete but is informed by visions that have a few key priorities and structures (Fullan, 1999). There are no single solutions. Pathways to success are virtually unknowable in advance of doing something, so schools have to craft their own actions by being critically reflective producers of change.

This transformative, collaborative view of change shuns both individualism and collectivism in favour of interrelationalism. Individualism is inappropriate in school development because of its inherent self-interest and its implicit isolation of people as decision-makers. Collectivism is also irrelevant because it implies that individuals have no power, a view that sits uneasily with liberal, notions of freedom. Interrelationalism is not a wet, reformatory compromise because unlike individualism and collectivism it is less concerned with outcomes than with the processes behind them, which is consistent with a whole school process-focused concept of EE/ESD (Foster, 2001; Sterling, 2001). While the value of individualism and collectivism lies respectively with the individual or the collective, the value in interrelationalism is in the *relationships* between people. Table 4.1 shows other significant differences between these three approaches.

Managing change in uncertain, uncharted waters

The management of change operates at the edge of chaos (Fullan, 1999), which means that schools have to adjust to a certain degree of uncertainty between too much and too little structure. The management practices needed to navigate this edge involve creating a culture of frequent change in a framework of few rules and activities. While being loosely structured these practices recognise that there are critical priorities in change, such as real deadlines and major outcomes (Fullan, 1999). What is offered in Table 4.2 are some guiding principles for designing and managing change based on the work of Fullan and Herz. As Table 4.2 indicates, transformative change encompasses a view that acknowledges that there are *de facto* leaders in schools. Realistically, these leaders discharge their duties in relation to change most successfully if they recognise that leadership of change can originate from anywhere in the school, including its pupils. In schools professing to develop whole school approaches the headteacher's leadership style would tend towards the democratic (Table 5.5).

Table 4.1: Individualism, collectivism and interrelationalism (Modified from Begg, 2000, based on Carter, 1990).

Feature	Individualism	Collectivism	Interrelationalism
Intrinsic Value	With the individual	With the collective	In the relationships between individuals
Direction	Individual autonomy	Individuals directed by the totality of collective, social forces	Individuals both self-directed and influenced by others
Development	Individual self-development	Self-development of the collective	Mutual development of individuals but not at each other's expense
Authority	Only from individuals	Only from the collective	From the relations between individuals
Responsibility	The individual is responsible for her/himself	The collective is responsible for all its members	Individuals responsible for their own destinies and those of others
Location of Moral Principles and Knowledge	Individual	Collective	Interpersonal relations
Explanations of Social Events	Individuals	The collective with its own laws	Inter-subjective

Change, organisational learning and interactive professionalism

Argyris and Schön (1996) identify two ways in which organisational learning occurs, single loop learning, which is concerned with accommodatory change and double loop learning with reformatory change (see Table 5.7). For example using quantifiable measures of added value rather than crude test scores is an example of single loop learning because it is seeking better ways of measuring success but still working within a platform of school effectiveness (see Table 4.3). The third phase of school development identified in Chapter One, which integrates aspects of school effectiveness and improvement is an example of double loop learning because this process involves modifying a platform by changing the ways in which school effectiveness and improvement are viewed (Table 4.3).

However the concept of collaborative, democratic change to whole school approaches to EE/ESD will require triple loop, transformatory learning at some stage (Table 5.7). Triple loop learning entails change that not only questions platforms but also critically interrogates an organisation's ultimate moral values and purpose and its educational ideologies (Table 4.3). For example, whole school approaches to EE/ESD would critically question

Table 4.2. Lessons and strategies for managing change: (Based on Fullan 1991, 1993, 1999 and Herz 1997 cited in Shallcross, 2004).

1. You cannot mandate what matters, the more complex the change the less you can force it. You cannot mandate local commitment and capacity but top-down mandates can constitute support for grassroots initiatives.

2. From monolithic to dynamic, alternative solutions. Change is a journey not a blueprint. Change is non-linear, loaded with uncertainty, and sometimes perverse.

3. Problems are inevitable; you cannot learn or be successful without them. See the opportunities that problems create. Times of crisis are good times to innovate.

4. Visions of outcomes and strategic planning come later. Premature or apparently unrealisable visions or plans can blind. Managers should think in terms of processes before objectives and visions.

5. You do not have to do it all alone. Move from innovations to institutional development, from going it alone, to alliances in which individuality and collectives have equal power in interrelationalism. You cannot have organisational learning without individual learning, and you cannot have learning in groups without addressing conflict. It is easier to enlist diversity to block action than it is to merge factions into a unified force of social change.

6. Neither centralisation or decentralisation work alone, both top-down and bottom-up strategies are usually required for successful change.

7. Connection with the wider environment is critical. The external is having a much greater impact on schools so schools need to collaborate with the outside to get the job done.

8. From neglect of, to the deeper appreciation of change. Everyone can be an agent of change . Change is too important to leave to experts. 'It is only by individuals taking action to alter their own environments that there is any chance for deep change' (Fullan, 1993: 40).

the assumption that humanity has greater value than nature. There is room for single-loop and double-loop learning in EE/ESD provided that these are part of a design strategy for change that is searching for a model for action that has transformatory change as its long-term aim.

> There is no contradiction in seeking to reform current ways of using nature while simultaneously seeking a shift toward a more inclusive level of awareness, in light of which nature would manifest itself as something other than an object for domination. (Zimmerman, 1988: 299)

Seeing learning, in this case single, double and triple loop learning, as contested professional activities is not a new concept in education (Postman and Weingartner, 1973; Giroux, 1996). However, contestation requires engaging with power-over strategies, not withdrawing from them, provided that this engagement avoids moral co-option into these strategies. So if EE/ESD is to be an action-focused, education as change, schools need to employ culturally critical situated learning not only as a key feature of their teaching of pupils but also of the professional development of their staff (Shallcross, 2004).

Interactive professionalism is a softer version of contested professionalism linked to interrelationalism and the notion of the *total teacher* (Fullan and Hargreaves, 1992). At its heart is the discretionary judgment that would involve contestation. This is professionalism based on:

- collaborative work cultures
- continuous improvement that seeks new ideas inside and outside the school
- reflective practices that honour individual and collective development
- greater mastery assessment, efficacy and satisfaction in whole school approaches to teaching

The individual guidelines for *total teachers* are to:

- locate and articulate his/her inner voice
- reflect in, on and about action
- develop a risk-taking mentality
- trust processes and appreciate others as total people
- work with colleagues
- seek variety but avoid fragmentation
- redefine his/her role to extend beyond the classroom
- balance work and life
- push and support headteachers and managers to develop interactive professionalism
- commit to continuous improvement and perpetual learning
- monitor and strengthen the link between personal improvement and pupil development (Fullan and Hargreaves, 1992)

This notion of interactive professionalism by interrelating individuality and collectivities into educational change sits well with the concept of whole school approaches (Chapter Two).

Designing sustainable change: an inclusive model of action for action

Whole school development is more successful if it employs an inclusive rather than deficit model of action that concentrates initially on what schools are achieving, rather than what they are failing to achieve. If such a model for action focuses on concrete decisions and actions, (Levels Three and Four in Table 4.3) rather than seeking consensus about ultimate values (Level Four in Table 4.3), there is a greater prospect of agreement about the shape of EE/ESD in schools.

Table 4.3: The four levels of influence on actions (Naess, 1995a)

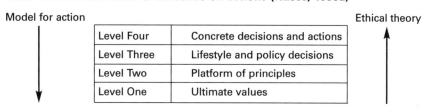

Model for action			Ethical theory
	Level Four	Concrete decisions and actions	
	Level Three	Lifestyle and policy decisions	
	Level Two	Platform of principles	
	Level One	Ultimate values	

This focus on inclusion is not a quest for an imposed or shallow consensus but for the recognition that when change is discussed at the level of ultimate religious, political or ethical values, perspectives often conflict (Level One in Table 4.3). However, when such discussions focus on action and agency (Levels Four and Three) there is greater prospect of agreement and consequently a more realistic model for action for schools (Table 4.3). This focus on action rather than on ultimate values means that teaching and other school staff often 'concur with the practice even though they operate from diverging theories' (Naess, 1995a: 66). Therefore, it is important that those who manage change do not privilege their own educational, environmental or ethical philosophies but regard their own values as one of a number competing perspectives that have to be considered.

An inclusive model for action starts by considering the social and organisational processes needed to implement concrete decisions and actions (Level Four in Table 4.3). Not only does this approach engage with the daily realities that school staff and pupils experience but it is often easier to reach agreement about what the appropriate educational processes are in schools than what constitutes a sound educational philosophy. Focusing on processes generically and outcomes locally offers the prospect of wider agreement and swifter action. This concern with action reflects the urgency Schumacher expressed about getting down to work and refraining from asking whether we will get there or not or which is the correct route (Orr, 1996). The environmental crisis is so urgent that action needs to be valued more highly than

71

intellectual conflict or debate although such conflict and debate will occur when actions are deliberated (Wilson, 2002). The best focus for action for most people is going to be their immediate environment and/or local community.

Evaluation comes first when deliberating and deciding on sustainable actions. A school could use organisational analysis to establish where it is (Argyris and Schön, 1996). This process involves internally organised surveys of existing practices, conditions and values. It cannot rely solely on the external measurement, evaluation and judgment associated with the school effectiveness agenda (Hargreaves and Hopkins, 1991) (see Chapter One). However, in the early stages of a model for action it may be advisable to adopt school analysis based on pluralist action research strategies. These strategies use quantitative and qualitative methods to illuminate the educational and environmental aspirations of all the stakeholders in the process of school development (see Chapter Five).

It is important that this inclusive model of organisational analysis demonstrates whenever possible that whole school approaches to EE/ESD are capable of meeting effectiveness standards. Integrating a qualitative approach to evaluation with one based on quantified standards should stimulate deep questions about the nature, purpose and ultimate values of an education such as ESD that seeks to realise sustainable development by working towards transformed lifestyles. A rigorous, critical, pluralist approach to surveying, based on action and participative local democracy, will fortify the knowledge, insight and commitment of teachers and pupils. This approach should mean that the data that schools disseminate to non-participants about whole school processes, including governmental bodies, is regarded as robust (Uzzell *et al*, 1994).

A first step on the road to whole school development is to appeal initially to short-term economic self-interest. It is often easier to focus on an issue, such as energy conservation that saves money but also makes a small contribution to the reduction in greenhouse gas emissions. Action would do well to start with short-term, economically-focused win/win actions as these can reduce inefficiency, produce greater resource efficiency, buy time and by invoking economic self-interest, the commonly held motive for socio-economic change, minimise potential social conflict. The financial motive will probably appeal more to the adults in schools such as governors and business managers while the environmental benefits of emissions reduction, no matter how small, would be their primary appeal to pupils. The pro-

72

cesses of deliberation and implementation should privilege small-scale practices (Evans, 1993) because even though success in EE/ESD requires long-term, sustained effort 'proximal sub-goals are needed to provide incentives and evidence of progress along the way' (Bandura, 1986: 453).

Advocating processes that lead to locally decided outcomes is also apposite because ESD in particular is at the stage of putative genesis. Visions of what the sustainable outcomes of process-focused, participatory ESD might be vague. This is another reason why design takes priority over vision, as design is often a long-term process of organising resources, not necessarily to realise a vision directly but to create the conditions in which achieving a vision is more likely (Begg, 2000).

EE/ESD has to integrate rigorous philosophical rationales for action with practical actions that apply these rationales in ways that are sensitive to, and deliberated in, local contexts. This approach may attract teachers because of its links with situated learning. Initially the intellectual appeal of a model for action could be to question the moral notion that humans are of sole value or of greater value than nature. Many school staff in Europe would currently identify with this idea, as it forms the root of much European philosophical and religious thinking. In the longer term opportunities will emerge to consider more environmentally focused philosophies and the types of sustainable actions that are congruent with these philosophies. Some environmental values will emerge as whole school approaches develop but the transformation to a situation in which environmental philosophies form the foundation for societal sustainable actions (see Table 4.3) is a very long-term process. However, this focus on education as action should not marginalise cognition, education about the environment and sustainable development or values education; education for sustainable development. Instead both knowledge and values education should be recognised as necessary but insufficient to achieve whole school education as sustainable development.

The integration of the three spheres of sustainable development (Figure 4.1 a or b) in whole school approaches is a vision for EE/ESD. Such a model is mapped in Figure 4.2. At the design stage of a programme of action in EE/ESD, schools would map their existing provision in the matrix shown in Figure 4.2. The three spheres of sustainable development feature at three levels: education about, for and as sustainable development. Alternatively, these three levels could be considered as the curricular, institutional practice and school culture including community links and evaluation. This second classification of levels may be an attractive approach to schools in which these three strands are distinguished within distributed leadership responsibilities. This occurs for example, when a school has a director of studies and middle managers responsible for curriculum leadership, a school business manager responsible for institutional practices and a headteacher leading socio-cultural development. Completing Figure 4.2 would ensure that the process of whole school development in EE/ESD commenced with evaluation. A journey to a relatively unknown destination becomes more dangerous if its point of origin is unclear.

Figure 4.1 a and b: Two views of the three sectors of sustainable development

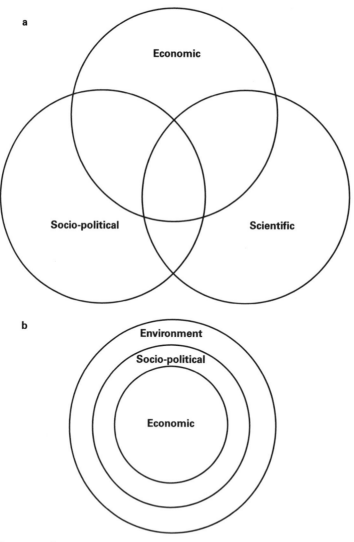

Do these two diagrams create different impressions of the nature of sustainable development? Are the concentric circles in (b) in the right order?

If for example, EE/ESD in a school was mainly taught at a cognitive level, in biological science, provision would lie in the scientific sphere at the about level (see (a) in Figure 4.2). Even schools which did not associate themselves with EE/ESD would find aspects of their practice that lay in at least one of the three spheres at this about level. The question that arises in relation to the management of change is not fundamentally about where current educational provision lies but whether those designing change in schools see whole school approaches as their vision, rather than a more limited focus on improved environmental awareness

Having established that EE/ESD provision is operating mainly at the level of education about the environment or sustainable development in the eco-logical sector, the question would be what is the next step in the school's design for future change? There is no single answer, as this decision will depend on information revealed by evaluative research, among other things, particularly that relating to the educational ideologies of staff, the agent of change's understanding of local context and other pressures on the school for change. For many schools the ideologies of staff may have a strong focus on human rather than natural interests and on a subject-based curriculum. External inspection is likely to reinforce these ideologies by putting schools under significant pressure to improve attainment through improved test scores. In this situation the school may decide to expand into other spheres of education about sustainable development, such as the social on the way to greater cognitive integration in the school curriculum (see Chapter Two).

Figure 4.2 offers a framework for mapping design from current provision by identifying the next steps in whole school development. Position (a) shows a school in which the current approach is education about sustainable development mainly taught through ecology. The next step, at this cognitive level, (position a1) might be to address teaching about global or national poverty or fairtrade. The action plan might identify teaching about the moral and/or religious issues raised by environmental problems as the next step (position a2). Moves into segments of increasing conceptual overlap could be justified in terms of citizenship or other cross-curricular agendas within the school curriculum. The school might develop strategies to move to the *for* or affective level by introducing values education strategies such as role-play in one or more of the three sectors, while recognising that its ultimate vision would be education as sustainable development rooted in collabora-tive, participative democratic education. A school could develop initiatives at more than one level at the same time.

Emergent changes will influence this journey. For example an issue may arise in school such as graffiti or bullying, or from outside school such as the promotion of healthy eating, that may deflect the intended path on Figure 4.2. These deflections may influence a school or teacher to consider pursuing paths from cognitive to affective and then active levels within one sphere, such as the scientific or social, at the same time. These may be the only paths open to a Science subject teacher or teachers who wish to develop the EE/ESD agenda in a school that is not engaging with these concepts at a whole school level. This solution would not be whole school EE/ESD but EE/ESD in a sustainable classroom or subject department that might be the precursor to whole school development. It is not only teachers who become drivers of this process, school support staff and pupils can become leaders particularly in the fields of institutional practice and community links (see Chapter Seven).

Figure 4.2: Education about sustainable development: starting points and pathways (Shallcross, 2003)

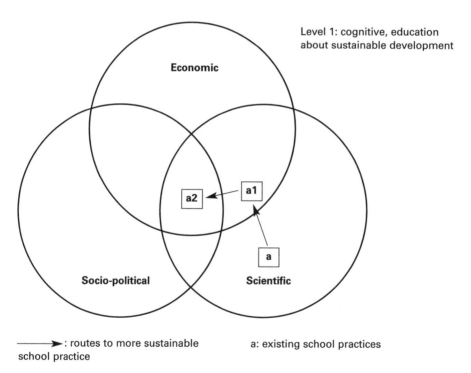

The eventual vision would be to achieve practices that integrate all three spheres of sustainable development at all three levels: education about, for and as sustainable development. However, this model for action seeks not to exclude by default but to include through design, by accepting that to some extent a school is practising EE/ESD even if it is operating in only one sphere at level one: the about level. The model shown in Figure 4.2 is more descriptive than it is analytical but its construction as an inclusive model facilitates both diagnosis and prognosis.

It is important that school staff use analysis as well as maps to identify the nature and quality of the social processes that underpin the destinations and pathways shown on Figure 4.2: these processes form the core of whole school approaches (see Chapter Two). These qualitative questions need answers from within the school, hence the importance of action research and evaluation that includes pupils as researchers in whole school development (Fielding, 2001) (see Chapter Three). Networking between schools at various levels of whole school EE/ESD provision will assist all the schools involved to develop the stamina to continue the journey towards their own vision of whole school EE/ESD provision.

A school-focused model of in-service or continuing professional development (CPD) (see Chapter One)

Whole school approaches are unlikely to be realised in many European schools without professional development support. Problems occur if centralised, top-down CPD is used as the only support for whole school development in EE/ESD. Centralised CPD involves individual school staff attending courses run at teacher education centres or institutions of higher education. Such centralised approaches often see change as externally driven and fail to consider how institutional factors in schools influence change, let alone equip school staff with the skills to manage change within their own schools (Fullan, 1991). In some narrower content or methodological areas, such as the teaching of reading, where the impetus for change focuses on the classroom teacher, centralised approaches may be successful. This top-down approach to CPD was used with some success to support the introduction of the National Literacy and Numeracy Strategies in England. However, in school development in EE/ESD, where the whole school is the focus and locus of change, it is a model with severe deficiencies (see Table 4.4).

The object of school-focused CPD in EE/ESD is the local development of the whole school (Evans, 1993) by not only training trainers but also by providing them with support materials than can be adapted for their local situations. For school development in EE/ESD to be authentic (Uzzell *et al*, 1994), schools also need to be more fully integrated with their local communities

Table 4.4: Some reasons for the failure of centralised CPD (modified from Fullan, 1991)

- One off workshops are widespread but ineffective
- Topics are selected by people other than those for whom the CPD is intended
- Follow-up support for ideas introduced through in-service occurs in only a small number of cases
- Follow up evaluation is rare
- In-service rarely addresses individual school's needs and/or concerns
- Most CPD programmes involve teachers from a variety of schools. These programmes often fail to recognise the different impact of positive and negative factors within the schools in which these teachers work
- There is a profound lack of a conceptual or theoretical base in the planning and implementation of CPD that would increase its effectiveness

and to make global connections from these local links (see Table 5.6). A school's educational improvement is clearly intended to benefit pupils, but we should remember that schools are also workplaces for teachers and support staff. School development can benefit several groups: pupils, teachers, support staff, parents and school boards or governors. Therefore CPD designed to promote EE/ESD needs to be contextually situated and relevant to the perceived and currently unseen needs, not only of school staff but also of others who are part of the school.

School-focused CPD is most likely to be successful if it integrates three knowledge bases (Figure 4.3):

- substantive, theoretical
- contextual, case study
- personal, experiential

For this reason theory, models and/or principles need to feature in school-focused CPD materials. By providing case studies alongside theoretical knowledge and principles, contextual knowledge can be analysed through the filters of theory and personal experience. Through a process of sensitive translation based on theoretical, personal and contextual reflection, or mirroring (Cassel and Giddens, 1993), teachers can make informed judgments about which aspects of case studies can be adapted for use in their own school, thus avoiding the uncritical copying or borrowing of ideas, which has been the reason for the failure of many innovations.

Figure 4.3: The three knowledge bases of CPD

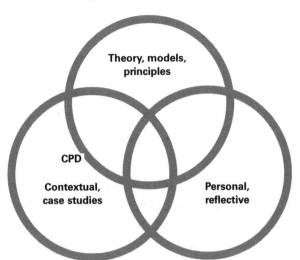

School-focused CPD offers solutions to many of the difficulties associated with centralised CPD (Table 4.4). This is particularly true if a school focus ensures that staff development creates individual and organisational habits and structures that make continuous learning a valued and endemic part of the culture of the school so that the school becomes a learning and organic organisation (Table 5.4). Besides creating the opportunity for locally derived action, a school focus also addresses the needs of schools and individuals. Hewton (1988) identifies two further advantages of school-focused CPD, of particular importance in EE/ESD. First, schools would identify and solve many of their own problems. Second, when schools are sufficiently motivated by their greater sense of control and autonomy, they will find the resources to support CPD.

However, simply basing CPD in schools can lead to problems such as the pooling of ignorance (Blenkin *et al*, 1992). Parochialism is a further problem that occurs when schools or individuals find difficulty in learning from the experiences of other schools or trainers. Another problem is that the resources and expertise of a school's staff can limit the range of CPD activities. A fourth difficulty is that CPD needs are frequently only internal to the school, resulting in a myopic focus that overlooks or neglects external circumstances (Hewton, 1988). School-focused CPD needs to illuminate those broader educational priorities that school staff may not perceive as needs, such as CPD in environmental ethics.

Devolving budgets to schools in some European countries makes school-focused CPD a pragmatic necessity but also raises other criticisms. First, many administrative tasks, such as routine departmental or staff meetings become part of CPD time. Second, schools are not necessarily adept at identifying long-term needs or needs relating to their local environment. Understandably, they tend to be preoccupied with the latest curriculum or inspection initiative from central government or strategies that will improve pupil scores in national tests. The most obvious conclusion that can be drawn from these observations is that geographically and contextually, CPD for whole school development in EE/ESD has to be school-focused and this process has to relate to the wider community.

Research (Shallcross *et al*, 2000) has identified three providers who stood out very clearly from the rest in providing CPD for primary schools in the U.K. These were, in order of importance:

- local government, mainly advisers or quality assurance personnel
- school staff, sometimes working in school networks
- radio and TV

The high profile of school staff as CPD providers, combined with concerns about the pooling of ignorance, is another strong argument for school-focused CPD because it trains trainers and provides them with the flexible resources and materials they need to run CPD programmes in their own schools. Chapter Eleven describes a European project (Shallcross, 2004) that promotes whole school development in EE/ESD.

Conclusion

Support, ranging from CPD projects to national and international networks or clusters of schools, is required to assist schools to navigate their way through change. The monitoring and evaluation of change against external criteria, such as good practice in other schools, revealed in case studies and normative models, can be a significant boost to an organisation's confidence. Without these external connections the motivation and progress of all but the most robust schools towards whole school development may evaporate.

As education has been a following discipline that cannot move ahead of economic policy, transformative whole school development will progress most successfully if it is linked to 'parallel change towards sustainability in wider society' (Sterling, 2001: 88). This vision of transformative change not only entails a more integrated view of educational change, it also implies change extending beyond the school gates to local or perhaps planetary communities, as does whole school development. But if education is a following discipline, does this imply that economic transformation must precede educational transformation?

It may be that the more whole school approaches incorporate transformed attitudes to economics, technology and governance in community-focused initiatives and address the predominantly social function of learning, the more education will be able to influence and eventually initiate the complex social changes that will lead to sustainable development in wider society. Thus whole school development may empower schools to become community leaders or catalysts of change to sustainable lifestyles at a community level (Uzzell *et al*, 1994).

SECTION B:
Case studies

5

Constructing case studies using evaluative research

Tony Shallcross, John Robinson and Arjen E.J. Wals

Introduction

This chapter examines the guidelines used to write the abstracts and in some cases design the research underpinning the case studies in Chapters Six to Ten. The template outlined in Table 5.1 was used to construct these abstracts. It is provided not as a blueprint but as an aid to the writing of comparative abstracts. The authors were encouraged to generate their own questions using the questions suggested under the case study headings in Table 5.1 as guidance. Using a common template to introduce each chapter makes it easier for readers to compare the widely differing contexts that are reflected in the case studies. The rationale behind these case study guidelines and some of the benefits and pitfalls of using case studies to promote educational change are discussed in Chapter Three.

Using case studies critically, analytically and constructively

The importance of contextual knowledge in professional development and school development was discussed in Chapter Four (see Figure 4.3). Case studies permit teachers and schools to learn from the negative and positive experiences of their peers. One reason for including section seven on constraints and difficulties in Table 5.1 is to avoid case studies being purely celebratory and the research design outlined in Section C is included to assist authors and schools to analyse the processes as well the hard data their research reveals. Exposure to the difficulties and problems experienced by others can be a valuable form of learning.

85

The case studies selected do not represent best practice. Authors chose case studies because they had direct personal experience of the schools they have written about. While some schools have been working on whole school development for many years, (see Chapters Six and Seven), others are closer to the start of this process (see Chapters Eight, Nine and Ten). The studies were also chosen to illustrate a range of contexts into which ideas about whole school development, in EE or ESD[6] are being introduced. For example there are significant differences in national systems of school evaluation. In Finland (Chapter Seven), there is a strong emphasis on internally driven self-evaluation, whereas external teams of inspectors have traditionally evaluated English schools (Chapter Six). Although the English system is moving towards more self-evaluation, the self-evaluation system schools have to use is still externally designed and moderated by the Office for Standards in Education (Ofsted).

Best practice is a problematic concept. Educators often disagree about what best practice looks like depending on their views about the purposes and processes underpinning good education. Best practice and visions of best practice can also disempower. To suggest that schools should try to develop fully integrated whole school approaches (see Figure 2.1) from scratch represents a major transformation in practices and perceptions for many teachers and schools (see Chapter Three). This will appear difficult, if not impossible, to many teachers (McCluney, 1994), so that whole school visions may seem interesting but irrelevant for addressing routine educational issues in their school:

> Call someone's entire way of life into question, and what you are apt to produce is defensive rigidity. It is elementary psychology that those who wish to change the world for the better should not begin by vilifying the public they seek to persuade, or by confronting it with a task that appears impossible. (Roszak, 1995: 16)

These guidelines were also used to construct the case studies contained in Unit Seven of the Sustainability Education in European Primary Schools (SEEPS) Project (Shallcross, 2004) (see Chapter Eleven for a more detailed description of this project). These case studies can be found on the Educating for Sustainable Futures website (www.education.ed.ac.uk/esf)

A model for self-evaluative research
The research model outlined here was used as a guide for research into the processes underpinning the case studies in Chapters, Six, Eight and Nine. This research model has four major aims. To identify:

86

Table 5.1: Guidelines for the writing of critical, analytical, case studies

1. Description of the School

- Age range and number of pupils

- Location

- Distinguishing features

2. Aims and Outcomes of the Project

- What are the main aims and intended learning outcomes of the project?

- Is the project subject based, linked to personal and social education and/or extra-curricular?

- How does the project link into a whole school approach?

- How many pupils are involved and across which age ranges?

- Is the project mainly a curriculum, institutional practice, social, evaluative or community project?

3. The Project: Content and Development

- What are the main content areas addressed by the project?

- How does the project respond to learners' needs? How does it respond to different learning styles?

- What competences and skills are developed through the project?

- How does the project respond to the school's needs?

- How does the project respond to the needs of the local community?

- Does the project promote active learning?

- Does the project address equity/ethical issues?

- Are the learning experiences problem based/experiential?

- Is the approach adopted integrated across subjects i.e. holistic? Does it promote systems thinking and practices?

- Does the project create space for critical reflection?

- Does the project require the pupils to act on information?

- How far does the project adopt a whole school approach?

- Is teaching on the project mainly didactic, discursive or active?

- How far does the project allow for pupil participation and the voice of pupils?

- How far does the project address citizenship and sustainability issues?

- Does the project present concepts (e.g. citizenship or sustainability) as fixed or negotiable concepts?

- Does the project encourage multiple perspectives?

- How far does the project address the development of values?

- How far do pupils and adults involved in the project act on the knowledge attitudes and values developed through the project?

- What resources are needed to develop the project? Were these available in the school at the start of the project?

4. Drivers: a) External b) Internal

a)

- Is the project linked to any external initiatives?
- Does the development of the project involve any external partners?
- What are the external reasons for getting involved in the project: LEA, marketing, community links, National Curriculum or national guidelines?
- Who from outside the school influenced the school to become involved in the project?
- How far were parents and other members of the local community involved in the decision to develop the project?

b)

- How does the project meet the educational philosophy of the school?
- Who within the school initiated involvement in or development of the project and for what reasons?
- Which school or community needs are addressed by the project?

5. Assessment

- How is cognitive gain assessed in the project?
- How are attitudes and attitudinal change assessed in the project?
- How are the actions of pupils resulting from the project assessed?
- Is assessment formative or summative?

6. Evaluation

- How is the quality of the project assured?
- Is project evaluation formative or summative?
- Are pupils,' teachers' and other adults' opinions sought about the project and valued?
- Is there evidence of any networking? How much of this is local/national/European/global?
- Which models, theories or approaches to change are adopted in the project?
- Were the strengths of the process identified and used to develop and implement the project?
- How do the outcomes relate to the intended outcomes of the project?

7. Constraints or Difficulties in Developing the Project

- What do those involved see as the main constraints or difficulties in initiating and developing the project?
- Have these constraints or difficulties been overcome and if so how?

8. Benefits of the Project

- What are the main benefits of the project?
- Which of these were foreseen and which emerged during the project?

9. Future Developments

- How will the project develop in the future?

10. Additional Comments

- Any points that you would like to make about the project that are not covered in the other sections?

- barriers to the implementation of whole school approaches to EE/ESD
- strategies to overcome or dissolve these barriers
- aspects of school culture and ethos which assist the development of whole school approaches to EE/ESD
- the benefits of whole school approaches to EE/ESD

The research methods employed are pluralist-based in the belief that specific research methods are not the preserve of any particular educational ideology such as school effectiveness or school improvement (see Chapter One). This model also recognises the need to provide empirical information to support the case for whole school approaches to EE/ESD; what can be quantified has significant political credibility within many European educational systems. Pluralism is also partly based on the beliefs that methodological distinctions between qualitative and quantitative approaches to research are often ones of degree rather than kind and a pluralist approach also assists triangulation or cross-checking between different respondents or sources of data. 'All quantification involves judgement as to qualities and all qualitative statements invoke hierarchy, number and amount to give shape to meaning' (Davies, 1982: 290).

One problem with interviews conducted in a micro-cultural setting such as a school is that the research cannot always ascertain whether the values that people claim to hold are mirrored in their own or their institution's actions (Posch, 1993). Quantitative audits of a school's physical environment provide empirical data that reveal insights into the consistency between the values that school staff and pupils profess to hold and the actions of their school. Interviews with different people associated with the school such as school staff, pupils and parents assist in cross-checking between groups and individuals about how they perceive not only their own levels of participation but also that of other groups in decision-making and action.

The first research area (Table 5.2) contributes to a contextual or situational analysis of a school in relation to its conceptions of EE/ESD. The second research area (Table 5.2) is an analysis of the school's policies, self-evaluation report (HMI, 2001) and recent external inspection report, if these exist. The view that EE/ESD is just another cross-curricular theme is an established barrier to its implementation because it is then perceived that EE/ESD must be evaluated in these terms. Thus EE/ESD means more work for already overloaded teachers. A more productive strategy is to view EE/ESD as good education that shows up positively using existing inspection evidence (HMI, 2001) or other quality criteria and indicators (Breiting, *et al*,

2005). The strength of the indicators produced by Breiting *et al*, is their process rather than outcomes focus. The search for individualised outcomes-focused performance indicators for EE/ESD may be a self-defeating strategy because comparing outcomes is difficult when they are being decided by schools in response to local issues and priorities. The uncertainty surrounding the identification of sustainable outcomes discussed in Chapters Three and Four exacerbates this difficulty.

The third research area (Table 5.2) is an audit of the school's physical environment and continues the contextual or situational analysis. One objective of whole school development could be the design of a survey of those areas of institutional practice that can involve pupils as researchers (Fielding, 2001), a crucial dimension of democratic education (Hart, 1997). The first three research areas, besides contributing to a situational analysis, also provide a partly empirical baseline against which the effects of the implementation of whole school approaches can be judged.

The fourth, fifth and sixth research areas (Table 5.2) are the heart of the cultural research. Researchers should consider the factors that influence school cultures if they are constructing interview schedules to investigate these three areas. These factors include:

- teachers' beliefs in childhood and how children should be treated
- headteachers' leadership styles and management skills
- the number, age range and background of children
- the communities schools serve
- the physical setting and resources available to schools (Adapted from Littledyke, 1997)

Interviewing is the most appropriate method for revealing the way these factors interact to influence the organisational culture of schools. 'The interview, therefore, is not just a device for gathering information. It is a process of reality construction to which both parties contribute and by which both are affected' (Woods, 1996: 53). Interviews with adults will often be individual, semi-structured or open. It is a good idea to give respondents the questions before semi-structured interviews to give them a greater opportunity to consider their responses.

Group interviews are probably the most appropriate strategy for research with pupils on their level of participation in school activity and their perspectives on the culture of the school (Ball, 1985). Citing Davies, Ball suggests that '.... the use of group interviews, actually provided for a re-creation

Table 5.2: A pluralist research model for the evaluation of whole school approaches to EE/ESD

Area	Objective/s	Target/s	Instruments
1	Investigating adults' conceptions of EE/ESD and whole school approaches	Headteacher, teaching and support staff	Interviews, semi-structured or open
2	Examining the school's policies, official annual external or internal evaluation reports	School staff, parents and other adults in the community	Reports and policies examined using content analysis
3	Survey of the school's environment	Institutional and social practices in the school and its grounds	Using an environmental audit
4	Investigating the school's social organisation	Teaching and support staff other adults involved with the school	Semi-structured or open interviews
5	Investigating the degree of pupil participation in decision-making in the school	Teachers and pupils	Semi-structured or open interviews
6	Investigating community links	Parents and other adults involved with the school who are not school staff	Structured, semi-structured or open interviews

of the relationships, cultural meanings, standards, roles and beliefs that constituted the active, living culture of childhood' (47). But interviews can also pose problems when used with children:

> For much of the age range we were interested in, children find it difficult to think and interact at a propositional level. That is, the more abstract the discussion, the less it means anything to them. .... In order to persuade children to reflect upon their experiences, interviews need to be embedded in more concrete realities. (Sanger *et al*, (1997): 191)

Adults have the experiences and cognitive images that will allow them to envision highly participatory schools, even if they do not believe they work in one. However, the question of children assessing their own participation is a significant design issue. For many pupils high levels of participation in school will be hypothetical (Davies, 1999). Hart's (1997) classification of levels of children's participation (see Table 2.1) provides a useful but not infallible analytical tool with which to compare children and adult responses. However, the difficult question is how can children imagine participation, where are their images of participation to originate from? How are we to make the concept of participation seem concrete when for many pupils this is not a reality in their schools? Trying to analyse levels of participation from their perspective is thus problematic (Council of Europe, 2000).

This fifth research area is potentially the most difficult of the six because it requires an understanding of those parts of the world which are central to children's construction of knowledge and to which adults are not privy (Ball, 1985). One solution is to use images to stimulate discussion, partly because children learn how to read images from an early age (Sanger et al, 1997). Before interviewing pupils they could view a video recording of children involved in a highly participatory school (OECD, 1993). Alternatively, line drawings showing whole school EE/ESD practice could be used during the interviews. Children can then be asked to compare their own experiences with these visual stimuli.

The integration of the six research areas clearly results in a pluralist research design that should produce thick description '..... which in contrast to straightforward description of facts, gives the context of an experience, and reveals the experience as a process' (Denzin, 1994: 505).

The research design (Table 5.2) also has a triangulation element. From a democratic perspective, the views of all other stakeholders in a school beside school staff are pertinent and should be a cross-referenced with the views of school staff. The use of policies, inspection and self-evaluation reports often provide a perspective from other people, often with a strong external interest. These sources also frequently use a generic template (HMI, 2001) that facilitates comparison between schools. Auditing school's physical environments provides a third cross-reference and a more empirical stance and interviews with children and parents provide other perspectives. By using these different research approaches the research design is more likely to reveal technological, artistic and communicative aspects as well as the sociological components of a school's culture.

The final aim of this research model is to develop community problem-solving action research skills among school staff, pupils and local communities (see Chapter Three). In this way schools acquire research skills that can be used to monitor the changes associated with the development of whole school approaches. This can be done through one of a number of potential action research cycles shown in Figure 5.1 by schools generating their own questions and analytical frameworks. Adopting one or more of these cycles also ensures continuous critical evaluation of a school's model for action (see Chapter Four).

The analytical categories provided in Tables 5.3-5.7 should not be seen as fixed. Schools should be encouraged to use other categories or classifications if they feel that these are more appropriate, or even establish their own analytical categories or classifications as these emerge from the research data. The analytical categories in Tables 5.3-5.7 are provided to help schools to report their conclusions through a common framework, not to provide an analytical blueprint. Suggested interview questions have been provided for the same reason. These questions and approaches have been field-tested. You can make your own judgment about the need for pluralism advocated in this chapter.

The model in Table 5.2 has not been referred to as an action research model as its use, in the form presented in Table 5.2, would represent an externally derived, internally administered approach to research, which does not have the degree of self-generation or self-reflection for the type of action research advocated in Chapter Three. However, Table 5.2 provides a model a school could adapt or transform so that resultant evaluation approaches would have a strong action research dimension.

Figure 5.1: Potential action research cycles (see Chapter Three) using the pluralist methodology shown in Table 5.2

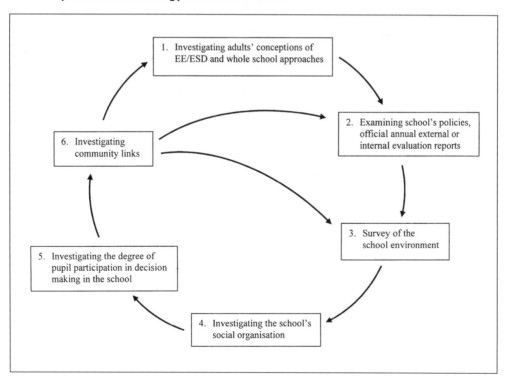

The following lists of suggested questions and analytical tools can be included in interviews to investigate five themes:

- school staff views on whole school development and approaches to EE/ESD
- pupil participation, questions for adults and questions for pupils
- school culture, leadership and change
- community links
- types of change

Suggested interview schedules

Teachers and other school staff
Suggested questions

- Do you believe education changes attitudes? If so how?
- Would you try to influence change in your school? If so how?
- Is it important that schools follow socially and environmentally friendly practices?
- Would you like to see more socially and environmentally friendly practices in your school?
- Does your school use its buildings and its grounds to teach EE/ESD?
- How do you teach EE/ESD in your school?
- Does your school practice a whole school approach? If so, what evidence is there to show that this is being carried out?

Analysis

Is the teacher or other member of school staff who has been interviewed, an activist, an attentive or an apathetic in relation to change?

1. Activists are always involved in trying to change things
2. Attentives are only involved in change when issues arise
3. Apathetics could not care less.

Which of the six descriptions of teachers listed in Table 5.3 fits your interviewee best?

Table 5.3: Teachers' roles in relation to social/environmental change (Shallcross, 2003)

Relationship with change	Characteristics
1. Instrumental	The social and natural environment is only of value as the place in which teaching takes place or which teaching is about.
2. Osmotic	Environmental concern comes naturally from outdoor experiences. Social concern results naturally from social contacts in schools. Specific teaching strategies for social and environmental change are not required.
3. Cognitive	Teaching is used to develop environmental and social awareness; social or environmental action develops naturally from this awareness.
4. Affective	Specific teaching strategies are used to develop social and environmental attitudes and values. Action is seen to result from values or attitudinal change.
5. Active	Specific teaching strategies are used to develop social or environmental action. Teaching is directly concerned with environmental change in the school and its grounds.
6. Integrated	Institutional actions, school culture, the formal curriculum, community links and evaluation are integrated in whole school approaches to social and environmental change. High-level pupil participation (Table 2.1) is encouraged within the school and its local community.

Children's participation
Suggested questions for adults

- Are pupils helped to express their opinions?

- Are pupils' views taken into account when decisions are made in your school?

- Are pupils involved in deciding about and engaging with their own learning or do teachers decide this?

- Does the school have a policy on pupil involvement in learning? If so, how was it arrived at?

- What barriers are there to the development of pupil participation in your school?

- Are pupils involved in making decisions about what is done in the school?

- Are there any differences in levels of pupil participation (see Table 2.1) across subject areas or classes?

- Do pupils and adults share power and responsibility for making decisions about the institutional practice and curriculum of the school?

- Are pupils and adults involved in changes in their local community?
- Are there any differences in levels of children's participation across the curriculum, institutional practice, social organisation, evaluation or community links?
- Does the school have a school council? If so who are its members?
- How do people become members of the school council?

Suggested questions for pupils

A video recording, photographs or line drawing could be used to stimulate discussion.

- What did you like in the video or the drawing of the school? What did you dislike in the video or the drawing of the school?
- Which parts of the video or the drawing of the school are like your school? Which parts are different?
- Is there anything in the video or on the drawing that you would like to see happen in your school? If so what is it and why would you like to see it in your school?
- How would you try to make these changes?
- What do you like about your school's grounds? What do you dislike about your school's grounds?
- What would you like to change in your school's grounds and why?
- How would you try to make these changes?
- What do you like about the inside of your school? What do you dislike about the inside of your school?
- What would you like to change in the inside of your school and why?
- How would you try to make these changes?
- What do you like about your lessons? What do you dislike about your lessons?
- What would you like to change about your lessons and why?
- How would you try to make these changes?
- What do you like about your local community and environment? What do you dislike about your local community and environment?
- What would you like to change in your local community and environment and why?
- How would you try to make these changes?

Analysis

On the basis of your interview decide the highest and lowest levels of children's participation (using Table 2.1) in:

■ the curriculum

■ institutional practices such as energy saving, development of school grounds

■ school culture and social organisation, such as school councils

■ positive changes in the local community

■ evaluating these actions

School culture, leadership and change
Suggested questions

■ How are major decisions made in your school?

■ How would you go about trying to influence change in your school?

■ Which aspects of your school's institutional practices are socially or environmentally friendly?

■ Describe the ethos or culture of your school

■ What are your school's development targets? How will these be achieved?

■ How strong are the schools' links with the local community?

■ Discuss the evidence that shows that your school is an organic/mechanistic organisation (Table 5.4)?

■ What style of leadership operates in your school (Table 5.5)?

Analysis of school culture
Table 5.4: Characteristics of mechanistic and organic organisations
(Based on Ogilvie, 1988, from Grieg *et al*, 1989)

Characteristic	Mechanistic	Organic
1. Structure	Hierarchical, top-down delegation	Flat, equal status, shared delegation
2. Policy, change and initiation	By the school's leaders, limited number of sources of change	Group agreement, change can start from anywhere in the school
3. Purpose	Collective, rather than based on individual potential; concerned with results	Concerned with individual potential, community based, concerned with people and processes
4. Control	From authority figures	Shared, based on group agreement
5. Communication	Limited, closed and within groups	Free, open and communal
6. Leadership	From the top	From anywhere as appropriate to the change
7. Membership	Limited and academic	Inclusive of pupils, support staff, community and parents

Analysis of leadership styles
Table 5.5: Leadership styles and their characteristics (Based on Ball, 1987)

Style	Characteristics
Interpersonal	Individually focused, based on informal chats, works through private persuasion and compromise, lines of power invisible
Managerial	Relies on structures, committees and working parties, ideas and planning are separated from practice, headteacher or the management team plan; teachers and other school staff do
Political/ Adversarial	Recognises that politics is a major feature of school life; relies on public meetings, open debates, public persuasion, talk and often challenge
Political/ Authoritarian	Recognises that politics is a major feature of school life; prevents the open discussion of other views, maintains the status quo, dislikes conflict; secret
Democratic	Collaborative culture based on persuading and including people, using open debate, councils and democratically elected groups, leadership may come from anyone.

Community links
Suggested questions

■ How are people and organisations from outside involved in the school? Name some examples

■ Who are the people involved in these links?

■ How is the local community and environment used by the school?

■ How does the local community use the school?

■ Is the school involved in any concrete actions in the local community? Give examples of these. Describe how these actions developed? What lessons can be learned for future projects?

■ Look at Table 5.6. Can you find examples of each of the school community links shown?

■ Which type of link is the most common?

■ Some writers think that level Four in Table 5.6 is essential if schools are going to develop authentic EE/ESD do you agree? If so how is your school going to develop this level of involvement? If you do not agree what do you think are the essential features of EE/ESD?

Table 5.6: School community relationships in EE/ESD (Adapted from Uzzell, *et al*, 1994)

Level	Sustainable development issues	Community school links	Action orientation
1. Isolated island	Dealing with real issues	Barriers	Developing action possibilities
2. Community as guest in school	Dealing with real issues	Removing barriers to EE/ESD in school	Developing action possibilities
3. School as guest in community	Dealing with real issues	Removing barriers to EE/ESD in the local community	Developing action possibilities
4. School as social agent	Dealing with real issues	Removing barriers to EE/ESD in the local community through pupil activity as part of the formal and non-formal curriculum	Concrete actions in the local community

Types of change

■ On the basis of the evidence that you have gained from these interviews decide which type or types of change are going on in your school; accommodatory, reformatory, transformatory or emergent (see Table 5.7)?

Table 5.7: Different types of change (Based on Sterling, 2001)

Nature of change	Characteristics
Accommodatory	The response of individuals or organisations to external decisions or events over which they have little or no control, for example finding the best way to implement an imposed change in the curriculum
Reformatory	This type of change would be critical of the links between existing practices and platforms but not of ultimate values themselves (see Table 4.3)
	Involves some element of individuals or organisations deciding for themselves to adjust the way they do things.
Transformatory	Takes place when individuals or organisations decide to do things in a different way that replaces many current practices This can be dubbed revolutionary change as it is based, at least in part, on new or revised platforms and ultimate values (see Table 4.3).
Emergent	The unexpected and unanticipated consequences of change. Decisions on small matters made by individuals, though apparently random, can together create the impression of coherent change
	This may establish a trend that people perceive as normal and hence influences their future decisions.

Conclusion

While all the case studies that follow in Chapters Six to Ten contain abstracts based on the guidelines outlined in Table 5.1, not all the case studies have adopted the research approach outlined in Section C. In the case studies which have adopted this approach, most of the research has been conducted under the guidance of an external researcher or researchers who are not members of the school staff. This may seem inconsistent with the internally driven, participatory and democratic approach to self-evaluation advocated in Chapter Three which produces open, self-determined and (co)created outcomes.

One reason for this discrepancy is national policy frameworks on school evaluation. In Nummenpää School (Chapter Seven) this internally driven, participatory approach to evaluation was entirely consistent with the open and flexible approach adopted by the Finnish Ministry of Education. Yet even in Nummenpää some approaches to evaluation were fixed by the agreement underpinning the COMENIUS proposal to which all participating schools had agreed. Whereas in other schools, such as Smallwood School (Chapter Six) in England, an open project approach to evaluation had to co-exist with a system of evaluation by inspection, largely orchestrated by institutions and individuals external to the school.

A second reason for the involvement of external researchers was the lack of research expertise in many of the case study schools. For each school to try to develop a participatory approach to action research independently and internally would have been foolish. The task of designing a self-evaluation model from within the schools would have been too difficult in isolation.

The integrity of involving outsiders and being involved as an external researcher depends on the action plan for future evaluations. If external involvement is a first step in developing the capacity for schools and their pupils to design and implement research, it is entirely consistent with the model for action outlined in Chapter Four. However, if this external involvement is associated with a form of research in which data is expropriated for publication and the school and its pupils only function is as a source of data then it is clearly not consistent with the research capacity building that is clear in most of the case studies.

In some cases a high degree of external or outsider research involvement can be illusory. In the Greek and Maltese case studies in particular (Chapters Eight and Nine), external researchers have been engaged in the school development process: this is partly why these particular schools were selected as case studies. So there is something of the insider, the action researcher (see Chapter Three) about the external researcher. They are not just observers of a school's development process, they are both participants and observers in it and because their participation precedes and exceeds their research role they can be described as participants-as-observers (Gold, 1958). However, participant observation has been challenged because of the methodological difficulty in balancing the subjectivity associated with being an internal participant with the objectivity brought by the external observer/ researcher. There is an alternative view that researchers cannot seek the Utopia of complete objectivity. Instead researchers need to recognise that all research and researchers are influenced by relationships that cannot be removed but can be known and acknowledged (Stanley, 2004).

Table 5.8: Key features of the six case studies: Chapters Six to Ten

Chapter	School name	Country	Sector	Size: no. of pupils	Main whole school strand	Secondary whole school strand	Distinctive features
6	Smallwood	England	Primary	125	Community links	Social, organisation school culture	Involvement with building a school in Somaliland
7	Nummenpää	Finland	Primary	30	Formal curriculum	Community links	International: European project
8	Second Primary School of Sykies	Greece	Primary	340	School grounds	Formal curriculum	Involvement of experts
9	St Theresa's Junior Lyceum	Malta	Secondary	1050	Institutional practice including school grounds	Formal curriculum	Extra-curricular focus
10	Vilarinho School	Portugal	Primary to lower secondary	26	Formal curriculum	Community links	International science project, strong focus on rural work

The final aim of the research model is to train school staff as action researchers who will subsequently evaluate the changes associated with the implementation of whole school approaches. Action research will also result in locally derived knowledge that can be used to support and develop teachers' grounded theories (Wals and Alblas, 1997). Currently action research features mainly in external courses which teachers pursue largely for career reasons: it is not a strong feature of the internal monitoring and self-evaluation of schools (Edwards, 1996). If whole school development is to lead to educational improvement, the research that evaluates this link has to involve as many stakeholders as possible. External experts do not know the whole story of the organisational culture of schools; they can only know a small part of it; teachers, support staff and pupils know much more. Internally derived action research in schools by schools should reveal this richer and deeper knowledge and so impart greater fidelity and verisimilitude to evaluative research.

In some of the case studies (Chapters Six, Eight and Nine) there are already signs of progress towards a more internally derived research model. After a first round of research, which included a staff development session to familiarise school staff about the research model outlined in this chapter, the researchers in each of these case studies are committed to further work with the school. This school development work helps to develop research capacity and in some cases pupils' roles as researchers (Fielding, 2001). In the Greek case study (Chapter Eight) there is already evidence of pupils being involved as researchers and in the Maltese case study (Chapter Nine) teachers have taken over some research roles for themselves. Table 5.8 identifies some key features of each of the case studies.

While advocating self-evaluation that is internally derived and applied, the benefits of involving external researchers should not be overlooked. They can often be sources of advice on alternative research paradigms. External researchers also bring with them the aura of detached objectivity that still impresses policy makers.

6

Being sensible and social sensibility: Smallwood Supporting Somaliland

John Robinson, Tony Shallcross and Pat McDonnell

Introduction

This chapter focuses on one particular project: *Smallwood Supporting Somaliland* which emerged from the process of whole school development in Smallwood Primary School in England. The headteacher is the charismatic driving force behind this whole school development and its links with the Somaliland project. Somewhat contrary to the whole school processes described in Chapters Eight and Nine, however, this chapter illustrates an emerging supportive collaborative grassroots culture in the school and amongst its pupils that is the key feature. This culture makes the *Smallwood Supporting Somaliland* initiative both possible and sustainable. While not principally designed as an EE or ESD⁷ project it clearly has features of EE/ESD (see Figure 4.2). This story shows that an international community link can help to stimulate whole school development. The case study also illustrates the greater space that exists for questioning and debate in a collaborative, participatory, quasi-democratic school culture.

Abstract

1. Description of the School: Smallwood Primary School, Cheshire, England is a small rural primary school of 125 pupils (four to eleven years of age) organised in four mixed age classes. The children come from a wide area that includes several towns as well as villages and local farms. Only about 27 per cent of the pupils live within the school's official catchment area.

2. Aims and Outcomes of the Project
Comparing the school and its community's standard of living with those of Somaliland inspired us to see the value of becoming involved in developing links with a culture and way of life far removed from our own. Since 2001 the school has:

- raised money for the Horn of Africa Learning Trust (HALT), a charity that supports the development of education in Somaliland

- helped to fund the building of a new school in Somaliland

Following a visit to Smallwood by the Prime Minister of Somaliland, separate links have been made with a hospital in Somaliland by some of the Smallwood parents who are health workers

3. The Project: Content and Development
The children have had direct experience at various levels, they:

- wrote letters requesting items and had to get used to the problem of occasionally being refused

- developed their performance skills so that they were able to act and sing in front of any audience

- had to negotiate the price of sending out a container and how much could go into it with a shipping company

- hosted a visit by the Prime Minister of Somaliland, along with several of his ministers and elders from the city in Somaliland where our partner school will be built

4. Drivers: a) External b) Internal
a) *Smallwood Supporting Somaliland* began with a chance encounter by the headteacher with a Somalilander living in England, the school listened to the story he told about the state of education in Somaliland, one of the poorest countries in Africa.

b) Smallwood was aware that multicultural education was a priority because its location means that the school has few pupils from ethnic minority backgrounds.

5. Assessment
Although the value of this project to the children cannot be measured, it should not be underestimated. We believe that it has influenced the way the children view their privileged position compared with the lives of other people and their understanding of their responsibility to try to change what they see as unfair or unjust.

6. Evaluation
We have always asked the children and parents about fund raising and several other charities are supported in school.

7. Constraints or Difficulties in Developing the Project
Perhaps the biggest problem is time management: children are called upon to sing/talk on a regular basis, often at the weekend. We had discussions with some parents who thought we should be raising funds for the school and for needs nearer home. We battled through these experiences by showing parents lots of video evidence, by inviting Somalis into school to give talks and through the help of supporters in the local community.

8. Benefits of the Project
Our children have a real sense of how they can help to change things. They understand their comparatively privileged positions, they are more likely to appreciate the differences that exist between people and to respect these differences.

9. Future Developments
The building of the new school in Somaliland commenced in 2004. There is also a commitment to ensure that it has trained teachers and to ensure its development. The headteacher would like to take some of the School Council members to Somaliland to see the work in progress. It is intended to run a course in the school to assist staff and pupils to take over the self-evaluative action research role themselves (see Table 5.2).

Research

The research methodology adopted for the data collection and sorting involved in constructing this account of the whole school approaches that led to the *Supporting Somaliland* project broadly followed methods described in Chapter Five. Evidence was gathered from the transcripts of thirteen interviews, including interviews with representatives of the four mixed-age class groups selected by the school, seven staff, including management, teaching, support and administrative staff, representatives of the School Council, which consists of two children from each year, elected by their peers, and a group interview with parents identified by the school. These interview data were supported by textual analysis of the school's policy portfolio, particularly:

- curriculum policy
- racial equality policy
- inclusion policy
- policy on working together and showing respect for staff and children
- Governing Body Review and Development
- the School Development Plan (SDP)
- a case study completed by the headteacher (Shallcross, 2004)
- a DVD produced by pupils

The following coding is used in presenting the data:

- Child: C followed by a number to indicate year group, C4 or School Council member: CSC
- Teacher: T
- Senior School Manager (Headteacher or Deputy Headteacher): SM
- Parents: P
- Support Staff (Administrators, Secretaries, Classroom Assistants): SS
- DVD: DVD
- the headteacher's case study (Shallcross *et al*, 2004): CS
- Interviewers: John Robinson (JR), Tony Shallcross (TS)

Many direct speech excerpts, especially from children, are included in the report on the findings of this research. This is intended to combat the danger of inauthentic reporting by researchers, who often unintentionally misrepresent what respondents, frequently children, say because they usually control what is written down. However, we realise that no matter how benign or democratic our intentions, our analytical and censorial power as researchers remains (Fielding, 2004).

Research findings

The context for the developments described in the abstract is contained in the school policies on working together and showing respect for staff and children, and the *Governing Body Review and Development Policy* (2001). This states that school procedures and policies should reflect the inclusive nature of education. *The School Development Plan* (SDP) is developed collaboratively by staff, children and parents. Thus the SDP is the end product of a long process of involvement and discussion (SM interview). The SDP focuses on developing approaches to inclusion (3) and encouraging ownership of school matters by raising the profile of the School Council (15). There is strong evidence in documentary and other research data of a general agreement that Smallwood applies a whole school approach to all aspects of school life (see Figure 2.1).

Two aims of the *Smallwood Supporting Somaliland* project were to enhance pupils' awareness of a culture other than their own and to contribute to their own citizenship education (DfEE, 1999). This has also been a lifelong learning experience for the pupils because they now have a better idea of the facilities that will exist for them when they are older. Children from Smallwood have given talks and made presentations to adults about multicultural

108

links. The project is cross-curricular, extra-curricular and community-based and involves the whole school community. Smallwood School decided to support educational development in Somaliland because only 10 per cent of Somaliland children receive any education at all, and only 3.3 per cent reach secondary education. Unemployment in Somaliland is extremely high, as are levels of poverty and disease.

Initially *Smallwood Supporting Somaliland* was a fundraising activity, but within a few months it began to penetrate many curriculum areas such as Art, Maths, English and Geography. Fundraising is one way in which the formal curriculum and institutional practices link local and planetary communities. Much of this fundraising has taken place out of school time through singing in shopping malls, washing cars, selling cakes at local factories and organising concerts in various venues. The funds have been used to send two containers to Somaliland containing 50 school boxes, each containing enough to establish a new bush school. In addition, the pupils raised money for 50 footballs which were distributed to children throughout Somaliland during Smallwood's official visit in 2003. Smallwood has also raised over £8000 for HALT (The Horn of Africa Learning Trust).

There are now regular joint Smallwood-Somali concerts, where each group performs for the other. Our children visit the local Somali community in England, eat Somali food, sing English songs and then dance Somali dances. The school has performed in Birmingham, Liverpool, London, Manchester and Sheffield, cities many pupils had never visited before. They have developed real understanding of the problems that foreigners, often refugees, experience when they live in England. And they have fun! Our experience of Somalilanders is that they like to cuddle and hug our children. The first time we take children to a Somali community in England, their English reserve is always apparent. But as the children quickly feel comfortable and safe, this apprehension soon disappears: you only have to watch the same child the next time he/she visits another Somali community.

Parents accompany their children on these visits and it is interesting to see how adult attitudes change as well. Hopefully these experiences will have a positive effect on parents' perceptions of other people and their problems and may make them more supportive, not only of domestic charities but those away from home. Smallwood has now established links with several other educational establishments who help by supplying goods, especially books that may be useful in Somaliland. While it would be easier for Smallwood staff to complete the paperwork for shipping these goods to

Somaliland, this would reduce the power of the project. The pupils benefit from having as much ownership as possible of their incursion into change.

Governors were keen to be involved in the project from the outset. One school governor, who is a trustee of HALT, has been on every visit to the different Somali communities in England. In 2003 the headteacher and the same school governor were invited to accompany a group of Somali elders, who live in the UK, on an official visit to Somaliland. During this official visit we were shown the site for the new school and had meetings with local elders. Two charities will oversee the building of the school and Smallwood has applied for UK National Lottery funding to help with the costs. The school in Somaliland will be called Smallwood.

The *Supporting Somaliland* project has also had significant impacts outside the school. The local university has established connections with a university in Somaliland and a parent in business in Cheshire has made a link with a business in Somaliland to explore the possibility of importing Somali ornaments. A local professional football club have sponsored a Somali football team from an inner city area in England and the club plans to go to Somaliland to set up football coaching programmes. Links have also been established between a hospital in Somaliland and health workers whose children attend Smallwood.

The project has developed significant relationships between the school and ethnic minority groups in the UK. It has contributed to achieving a major target of the school's *Racial Equality and Inclusion Policy* (2001) i.e. to develop the multicultural competence of Smallwood pupils, who are drawn very largely from the UK's white community. Multicultural competence requires the development of cultural awareness, knowledge, sensitivity and action. The *Supporting Somaliland* project illustrates how these four dimensions of cultural competence can be nurtured and extended through a whole school approach. It is also important to ensure that the *Smallwood Supporting Somaliland* project does not dominate the school's community links and that the school supports local community projects as well. Making connections with Somali communities in England has helped to make the connection with Somaliland more real and meaningful for everyone involved.

Supporting Somaliland has involved Smallwood pupils at various levels. The project now involves the whole school from the smallest four-year old to the headteacher and governors. It has become cross-curricular, extra-curricular and community-based, through the links made with ethnic groups throughout the UK. The project enables Smallwood pupils to understand much more about the world they live in. It reaches out to the outside world and brings the outside world into what is a generally a small, but diverse, relatively affluent rural community and school. However, Smallwood has a diverse pupil intake. A significant minority of its children are from somewhat disadvantaged backgrounds and 25 per cent of its pupils have special educational needs (SEN). The benefits of *Supporting Somaliland* are considerable; this diverse range of pupils have:

- written letters to various local businesses seeking items to be donated to the project and have had to deal with the problems of refusal
- acted and sung in front of audiences at various events in order to raise money
- developed their drama skills
- established regular joint Smallwood-Somali concerts as an extra-curricular activity
- visited local Somali communities in England, shared Somali food, sung English songs and danced Somali dances
- negotiated the price of sending a container from the UK to Somaliland and identified the capacity of a container with shipping companies
- calculated the budget needed to fill a school box
- become accustomed to bargain hunting
- developed an awareness of what it feels like to live as a refugee
- raised money to buy 50 footballs to send to Somali children

When asked about the school's democratic approach to classroom organisation that underpins the Somaliland and other projects and why this approach worked a teacher said:

> Because they're comfortable. They've had an input into it, it's their decision and they feel that if it hasn't gone right they're able to make a suggestion of how it can be improved, so it's all theirs, they've had an input on it, they've got ownership to it. (T interview)

When asked about parents' impressions of the school and the importance of academic results in attracting children, a member of the school support staff identified the whole school approach as a factor:

> I think initially it's probably results, especially for people moving into the area, and recommendations from other parents, I think it's the whole school – and Pat (the headteacher) – her philosophy transfers itself to everything about the school, the way she wants to teach children, and how she teaches children, just to be rounded human beings when they leave school. She likes

111

them to have as much human contact as possible, to be responsible human beings, and prepare them for what's to come in secondary school. (SS interview)

This view of the headteacher as the initial founder of this whole school culture, who had now become the bearer of this culture (Nias *et al*, 1989), was widely held by staff, pupils and parents. Class four pupils explained how they got involved in decision-making in the school. 'We were asked if we wanted a new classroom and new toilets'(C6 interview). Later they described how they had made a DVD showing different aspects of school life (C6 interview). Several of the interviewees, including representatives of the Senior Management Team, the School Council, pupils, teachers and support staff alluded to whole school approaches when they explained how parents were involved in the life of the school. The school policy documents reveal that changes to the learning and teaching regime for individual children will only happen after the parents (and/or carers) of the child have been consulted.

Everyone, I hope, has an equal voice in the school, down to the support staff etc. and a good example of that was last week when a mum came up and made a suggestion. I hope the parents know that it's their school as well and we've got to be receptive, if the decision-making is done by a group then you're more likely to get it accepted by everybody. Or most people anyway. (SM interview)

This quote illustrates not only a philosophical commitment to a democratic view of leadership and a collaborative view of decision-making but also pragmatic reasons for involving parents and carers in whole school decision-making. The involvement of parents and carers not only motivates them but also facilitates the process of change. The style in which this opinion is expressed implies that it was conscious decision in designing change as well as a visionary commitment (see Chapter Four). There appears to be a strong sense of belonging in the school, shared at all levels of the school population, which is underpinned by a policy which shows a sophisticated understanding of the pedagogical power of the non-formal curriculum. The interview data illuminates a strong synergy between policy and practice in the school:

The curriculum is all the planned activities that we organise in order to promote learning and personal growth and development ... It also includes the 'hidden curriculum', or what the children learn from the way they are treated and expected to behave. We aim to teach children how to grow into positive, responsible people, who can work and co-operate with others while developing knowledge and skills, so that they can achieve their true potential. (Curriculum policy)

Supporting Somaliland is clearly an important project for the school as the following reference in the School Development Plan shows:

> Links with other communities – to develop links with Somaliland and encourage a deeper understanding of another culture through fundraising, hosting officials from Somaliland and sponsoring a Somali football club in Manchester with Crewe Alexandra Football Club. (SDP: 22)

One interviewee felt that the *Supporting Somaliland* project demonstrated the strength of the school's community links:

> Very much so, yes, the entire community, I think certainly of the global community when you think of Somaliland. (T interview)

When members of the School Council were asked about what they had learned about Somaliland the *Supporting Somaliland* project quickly became a focus for the conversation:

> Well I think Somaliland deserves much more than they've got, all worn stuff.
>
> What about you M? (JR)
>
> I think the same as S. We've raised quite a lot of money for Somaliland – £40000. At the Cheshire Show we had a Teddy Tombola and the money from that goes to Somaliland and we also have this big bottle and if you have any loose change you can put it in the bottle.
>
> And what did you know about Somaliland then, what can you tell me about it? (JR)
>
> They've not got many schools and the schools they have got are like under trees. We've raised money so we can help them get a school and I think they're building one but need a bit more money.
>
> And is that something you are proud of? (JR)
>
> I am, I am. (CSC6 interview).

Supporting Somaliland works at Smallwood because it is collaborative and participatory, based on whole school principles that utilise the community focus that permeates other aspects of school life. It is not an adjunct, bolted on to school life but an extension of the direction the school has been taking for some time creating an ethos of collaboration, cooperation and involving all members of the school community. However, the headteacher acknowledges that the smallness of the school makes it easier to establish and maintain this ethos. The school's size has meant that it has faced the threat of closure twice during the present headteacher's tenure. As she says, a collaborative culture brings difficulties as well as blessings:

> We have 125 pupils, it's counted as a small primary school. I've worked in a very large (school), but the philosophy was totally different. Children were children and didn't have much part in decision-making, and parents had no part of it. It is easier in a small school because everyone does know each other, but when I first came here it certainly wasn't as it is now and the path hasn't always been very easy, we've had to talk to the staff a lot, who've had to be convinced that decision-making should be more democratic ... Parents can come and say anything to me as long as it's done in the right spirit and I'll accept it and say things back to them, you've sometimes got to suffer the consequences, and they are that you will get something that you don't like but that you will have to handle because you have stuck your neck out. You have to work through it.

> Did the children take much persuading? (JR)

> No. Not at all. It's an evolution, not a revolution. They like to be respected for what they say, and what they say, almost always now, is very sensible. (SM interview)

One of the major benefits of this collaborative approach is that teachers feel they have space to say what they feel, even when they disagree with the school's senior management. Support staff feel that senior managers are approachable. All the members of the school staff regard Smallwood as a school in which professional conversations dominate and where 'taking risks' characterises the school's approach to problem-solving (SM interview). These observations also illustrate the point made in Chapter Two that collaborative cultures foster a professionalism that encourages critique and argument because in a collaborative ethos school staff work in close social spaces (Pollard, 1985). As these and other extracts from the Smallwood research indicate, there is safety in these spaces to express the dissenting opinions that often become topics of staffroom complaint rather than formal discussion in more authoritarian school cultures (Nias *et al*, 1989).

Evidence from the DVD supports this collaborative approach. The DVD and research data indicate that Smallwood is an organic rather than mechanistic organisation, (see Table 5.4) with the highest levels of pupil participation (see Table 2.1). Management structures may be the least organic of the school's organisational features which is partly the consequence of the legal responsibilities placed on the headteacher and the school's governing body. However the interview data shows that most respondents see the headteacher as a visionary, heroic leader, even though this leadership is used to promote more open democratic approaches to schooling (Aspin, 1995; Beane and Apple, 1999). For example the school DVD is entirely fronted by pupils and pupils are involved as researchers (Fielding, 2004) in helping to design the annual pupil questionnaire about learning and teaching (SM interview).

While the headteacher does not see herself as a hierarchical leader, the overriding impression is that she is first among equals. Leadership, in the identification of initiatives in Smallwood, is organic and can originate from anywhere within the school community, including its pupils. The consensus is that the headteacher's leadership style is democratic, with strong interpersonal features (see Table 5.5), operating within a largely collaborative school culture. Two children interviewed a teacher about the value of a residential school trip (DVD), the teacher identifies the reciprocal impacts of this collaborative culture on the staff:

> We learn to work as a group. You learn to work with others. They see us (teachers), hopefully, as human beings. They see us in our pjs. You see us when we are tired. You learn to do different things with different people. Its gels us all together. (T interview on DVD)

However, when pupils were asked about their own participation in the life of the school they recognised the limits to their involvement:

> Do you think you should be able to say something about what you learn? (JR)
>
> Yeah. But not like art all the time, it's got to be sensible. (C6 interview)
>
> We have a suggestion box and we open it up every week and we read the suggestions and talk about whether they're sensible and stuff. (CSC interview)

One of the Year Six pupils said about the work of the School Council:

> We don't like just being told stuff, we like doing it, practical. If we think we're not doing enough of it, could we do more, we'd probably do more of it. If you're being stupid they wouldn't take any notice.
>
> Who decides if it's sensible? (JR)
>
> The School Council. [The headteacher] as well. If [the headteacher] doesn't think it's sensible it doesn't happen. (C6 interview)

What is interesting is the relatively ubiquitous use of the word sensible when the pupils are describing how decisions are made about what the school should do. There is a clear indication from pupils that the grail of common sense is the intellectual property of the headteacher. In what follows there is the suggestion that what is sensible becomes part of pupils' learning how to circumvent rejection. When we put this point to the headteacher she said:

> When we asked the children, nearly everyone said that the headteacher would listen to us if we come up with something sensible. (JR)
>
> I think that when I first started this and we started the suggestion box, you've got the usual things, which they determined themselves. They're not outrageous requests, they're requests from a child's point of view, and they work through that stage, because our idea of being sensible isn't their idea. You've got to remember that. (SM interview)

There is plenty of evidence that the school has developed a strong community-focused approach to learning and teaching. Parents have a significant involvement in many of the decisions taken throughout the school. Visitors are a daily feature of school life: for example locally based artists 'bring in their work and explain some of [it]' (T interview). The approach taken by the school to its healthy school initiative exemplifies the involvement of parents and children:

> I wanted to change the system where the children ate crisps and sweets at playtime. So I went to the children, and the parents, and we set up a committee that met initially about once a month, with governors, teachers, the School Council and me and the parents, to see how we could make the school healthier. And some ideas of serving breadsticks, not allowing crisps, we knew it would meet opposition (from the children) and it did, but because the parents were in on it they would defend our stance. (SM interview)

While this indicates that the community is actively involved in the school, *Supporting Somaliland* also shows that the school acts as an agent of social change (see Table 5.6). This agency is also illustrated by pupils educating their parents about healthy eating. S described how her father used to stop at a fast food kiosk to buy a bacon sandwich or burger for his breakfast on his way to work. After S explained to her parents what she had learned in school about eating a more healthy diet, her father began to eat a more nourishing and less fatty breakfast at home before he went to work (C4 interview). Another parent said that she took charitable donations much more seriously as a result of discussions with her daughter about *Supporting Somaliland* and other charitable projects the school had been involved with.

The teachers agreed that parents were significant partners in their children's learning and although involving parents was occasionally 'a bit time-consuming' (T interview), significant benefits followed because parents felt involved. The same teacher also spoke about asking parents for advice about the education of their children. Pupils also provided examples of their parents being involved in the life of the school. This included parental involvement in school clubs (C3 interview).

Although there seems to be a strong relationship between the changes established within the school and learning that accompanies these changes, not all the research data reflect a consensus over the ways in which the school operates. The following extract from an interview with one of the teachers illustrates both of these points as well as acknowledging the critical importance of linking messages from the formal curriculum with institutional practices:

> Can I just pick that point up about choices for lunch because it seems to me if that had come out where the kids were saying we want sausage, beans, egg and chips all the time and we want plenty of sweets there's a tension between that and... (TS)
>
> Absolutely, well that's where the education comes in beforehand.
>
> So when they actually made these choices were they choices that were very much pro healthy eating? (TS)
>
> I think these were choices made post-learning about what's good for you, certainly. That was at the top of their minds. This is where it all came from of course because that's what we were doing at the time and the discussion came up that we may be able to change school dinners in this way. Another thing was something simple like putting the choices on display for people to read as they come to the dining hall so they know immediately what they want instead of going looking and just picking up things. That was a decision of theirs as well but obviously there are changes in other certain aspects of eating lunch, which have to be controlled by the school because otherwise I'm sure there would be children who would love to have chips and sausages every day.
>
> What I'm asking you is the raw consensus...........was that pro-healthy eating in the main?(TS)
>
> It was pro-healthy eating in the main. Obviously they don't want to have their chips and things moved away but they're quite happy to sacrifice once or twice a week. (T interview)

This learning-led change, which the above extract suggests was a form of guided discovery, was recognised by the parents (P interview). On occasions pupils may be guided towards decisions that resonate with the direction the school staff would like to take. Thus children are socialised into aspects of practice. They are beginning to learn that there are parameters; that what goes on in school is subject to some degree of external and internal guidance. In the Smallwood context situated learning implies becoming sensitised to the sensible. But for one member of staff the involvement of children and parents has gone a little too far. The final point she makes may illustrate why staff see the need for the formal curriculum to act as a guide:

> I think the children have more say in the school than the staff, this school is run by the children, and the parents, and in other schools they do have a say, but here they do run the school.
>
> Do you think that's a good idea? (JR)
>
> In a way yes, and in a way, no. Yes: because it wouldn't be such a great school – it's a fantastic school to work in, I've never worked in another school but I've visited other schools, and I came to this school (as a pupil), looking back at that it has changed from going back seven to ten years when I was here, I didn't have the things that they have now (Coppice Club)[8]. If we raise some money the kids get to choose what we get for the school.
>
> So you said the children and the parents control the school, what's the negative side of it? (JR)
>
> We can't do right for doing wrong. We were talking in the staffroom, most of the parents are complaining that the children are having too much homework, so we go one step back, and now they're not having enough homework. You can't ever have a happy medium with them because they know best. Or they think differently, they don't all think the same. (SS interview)

Parents see Smallwood as significantly different to other primary schools in the locality. The school's openness to parents, its ear for children's voices and the richness of its extra-curricular life are some of the distinctive differences that parents identify with Smallwood. The headteacher put it differently. She does not want Smallwood to be seen as 'a SATs factory' (SATs stands for Standard Attainment Tests, national examinations that all primary school pupils sit in England when they are eleven years old). SATs results are one of the measures used to judge the effectiveness of primary schools and to rank schools in league tables. Even though Smallwood has been ranked as the top primary school in its LEA using this criterion, the headteacher shunned the publicity associated with this success because she is more interested in seeing the school featured in the local media because of the broader social and artistic achievement of its pupils. She is a strong believer that if pupils feel a sense of worth because they are consulted and participate this leads to achievement that spawns the self-efficacy and motivation (Bandura, 1986) which fuels high attainment.

Although Smallwood has twice been threatened with closure, the distinctive reputation the school has created for itself through its focus on whole school development has attracted parents to send their children to the school.

Smallwood is now oversubscribed and only 27 per cent of its pupils come from within the school's official catchment area. In recent years there have been extensions to the school's buildings and its immediate future seems secure.

Conclusion

This critical evaluation of the *Supporting Somaliland* project has illustrated ways in which this project has contributed to whole school approaches to school development at Smallwood School. There is clear evidence from the data that pupils are actively and positively engaged in their own and other's learning and actions. This learning and teaching has a stronger focus on the social and aesthetic rather than the environmental. In this respect teachers show an active or integrated approach to social rather than environmental change (see Table 5.3).

Though an example of good practice, this account is not offered so it can be emulated, borrowed or copied (see Chapter Three). It is included because it is illustrative of significant processes of developing a whole school approach with strong community links (see Chapter Two). We have highlighted some of the process and content issues that came up through this project. *Supporting Somaliland* does not set out how to do a Third World development project. Rather it is about how a school community has thought through an issue which has cross-curricular, extra-curricular, community and whole school connections that involve school staff, pupils, parents, governors and the wider Somali and Somaliland communities. *Supporting Somaliland* has had a significant impact on the planetary understanding of the pupils and their actions as global citizens.

Adult members of the school believe that the value of the *Supporting Somaliland* project to the children cannot be overestimated. Although such benefits cannot be measured, there is a belief in the school that the project has influenced the ways in which the children think about their comparative privilege, their perspectives on the lives of other people and their understandings of their own responsibility to seek to change what they see as unjust (CS). In short, this is active citizenship education. However, the project has also shown emergent features in the process of change, particularly in broadening and deepening parents' perceptions of other people's problems and aspirations (CS). One of us (Robinson, 2003) has reported elsewhere how 'teaching about the Third World' can fail if it does not adopt the cultural competence approach that *Supporting Somaliland* so clearly demonstrates.

However, some significant questions remain about *Supporting Somaliland*:

- In reality, whose project was it? Although it had a serendipitous beginning through the influence of the headteacher, serendipity only acts as a driver when the cultural conditions in schools are free and supportive enough to respond to it. This is clearly the case in Smallwood. However, the main driving force is the headteacher. Such projects may have problems of sustainability when personnel change.

- What will happen to *Supporting Somaliland* and indeed the whole Smallwood project when the headteacher retires? It is noteworthy that *Supporting Somaliland* was only mentioned in one interview with pupils on the School Council. The project did not figure in the DVD made by the pupils about the life of the school (SM interview; DVD). What did figure prominently in all the interview data was a profound sense of developing pupil self-efficacy (Bandura, 1986).

- The project also raises questions about what constitutes a community. Is it geographical, organisational or ideological or a combination of these properties? Strong claims are made about the impact of *Supporting Somaliland* in terms of developing community links within and outside the school. But as Burbules (2000) points out, community is not an object but a claim to knowledge which is wrapped up in the social conditions and practices of the society from which the claim originates. The claims about the community impact of *Supporting Somaliland* could be considered more closely from both Somali and Smallwood perspectives through some form of action research project, though this would create further pressures on time.

- The project also raises questions about what differences in vision exist between democratic and non-democratic schools.

The *Supporting Somaliland* project illustrates many of the characteristics of a democratic learning institution. The principles of a democratic institution include: equality, freedom, tolerance, consideration of other people's interests and respect for other people (Aspin, 1995). Smallwood's approach to whole school development and the *Supporting Somaliland* Project address these principles with integrity. However, there is little evidence in the data of pupil involvement in decisions about learning, teaching and assessment. The centralised control over curriculum content, assessment and to a lesser extent teaching in England may explain this limited involvement.

Smallwood's focus on a community links approach to whole school development in the *Supporting Somaliland* initiative goes a long way towards achieving a genuinely democratic approach to the project and to other aspects of school life. As in most, if not every school, visions are both malleable and illusory and they are subject to external and internal influences that render them dynamic. Even for schools as accomplished as Smallwood there are still initiatives to be taken and cogent reasons for prioritising some actions over others. The destination may never be reached but many transformations can occur on the journey.

Acknowledgement

We would like to thank all the staff and pupils of Smallwood School for being so helpful and cooperative and making us feel welcome in the school whilst we conducted this research. We would also like to thank the parents who contributed so enthusiastically to the research. We hope they enjoy the story.

7

Enthusiasm and the creation of meaning in individual work: the Three Es project

Hanna Niiranen-Niittylä with Tony Shallcross

Introduction

This case study is the story of how a small school in the Finnish countryside ran an international COMENIUS EE or ESD[9] project involving more than 3000 people, including pupils, teachers, parents and local authority officials from six different countries. While the chapter looks mainly at the impact of this project on Nummenpää School in Finland it also examines how the project affected the schools from outside Finland. There is particular emphasis on self-evaluation and community involvement in this case study.

Abstract

1. Description of the school: Nummenpää School, Paimio, Finland is a small primary school with 30 pupils, located in a rural area in South-West Finland. The staff consists of two full-time teachers, two part-time teachers, a cook and a janitor. The headteacher is only at the school once a week because he has another large school to manage. Consequently Nummenpää is independent when it comes to curriculum, development, everyday school life and pedagogical matters. The school caters for first to sixth grade pupils between seven and thirteen years-old.

2. Aims and Outcomes of the project

The Three Es *Environmental Education in Europe* COMENIUS project's main aims were to promote:

- the ideology of children as active, being citizens (John, 1996) deciding on and doing their own work for their own environment, this is EE not just as knowing but EE as learning by doing
- whole school approaches
- networking not only between the seven partner schools but within each school's local community

3. The Project: Content and Development

The project involved schools from Cyprus, the Czech Republic, Finland, Italy Lithuania and Wales. All seven schools cater for primary pupils and two have secondary pupils. All the schools shared the project's common values (see 2 above). In addition all the schools wanted to use the project to develop English language and information technology (ICT) skills. The title *Environmental Education in Europe* was chosen because the project represented: Nordic, Baltic, Central European, Western European and Mediterranean countries. The project developed environmental work between all the schools involved. It also developed international cooperation and understanding through visits and the use of ICT. Each year of the three-year project was divided into two or three periods and each period had a theme focusing on a specified environmental theme, such as water or waste. The project outcomes were many and varied, such as more sustainable ways of running institutional practices, new teaching methods the production of videos, CDs, articles, booklets and two public exhibitions of children's' art work on the theme of nature. Students training as classroom assistants helped the teachers at Nummenpää with the project.

4. Drivers: a) External b) Internal

a) The Finnish National Core Curriculum (Ministry of Education, 1994) and national and international teacher education courses in EE, including a COMENIUS course.

b) Nummenpää School's own curriculum design and the school's major commitment to sustainability values. The school explored the possibilities of establishing international contacts, with the headteacher's support.

5. Assessment

Teachers observed a noticeable improvement in children's ICT skills and attitudes and actions for the environment, such as fourth, fifth and sixth grade pupils learning to edit photographs. Some even analysed statistics using computer programs.

6. Evaluation

There was no common approach to evaluation among the project schools. Teachers' observations and open discussions were the main ways of evaluating the project in Nummenpää School. The project created a halo for EE that has a positive effect on children's, parents' and staff attitudes. The project attracted a lot of parental and community attention. Every family with a child in the school was represented at at least one of the project happenings; most attended several of these events. The evaluations at Nummenpää encouraged pupils to reflect critically on how the project could be improved.

7. Constraints or Difficulties in Developing the Project

Because the project was funded by COMENIUS, it had to be well documented both in its financial and programme details. Local authorities only showed interest in the project after it had secured COMENIUS funding and a lot of publicity. The project became larger than originally expected, which made it difficult to coordinate because of its size and complexity. Small schools like Nummenpää are in danger of closure in Finland but this threat was not mentioned during the project.

8. Benefits of the project
In 2002 the Paimio Local Agenda 21 Committee gave its annual prize to Nummenpää School. The school janitor had a particularly effective role to play in the project. The school got an extra member of staff for seven months who taught ICT, created websites and organised the school's Intranet. The project built networks with local and regional environmental authorities and workers.

9. Future Developments
Future co-operation between the schools in the project is under discussion. It is possible that many of the schools will explore the possibilities of becoming an Eco-school (see Chapter Eleven) or other national award programmes for EE.

Research

Project evaluation was formative: it was intended to develop cooperation and improve working methods in the project and was not meant to be highly analytical or scientific. Each school set up its own system of evaluation to suit its context and its local or national system of evaluation. The main aim of evaluation was to facilitate teachers' and children's teaching and learning about environmental issues and the subject matter of each theme. In practical terms this flexible approach to evaluation served the interests of both the teachers and children who were involved in the project.

The project has been evaluated by the individual schools and at COMENIUS project meetings involving all seven schools. The evaluation of each environmental theme in the project was formative, based on data collected from both teachers and pupils in each school. Open discussions were used to gather the opinions of both children and adults. Evaluations at the end of each year were both summative and formative. Data was collected from parents and pupils and others involved in the project in each school first, then summarised at a COMENIUS project meeting with all the schools. These feedback and evaluation results were also used to inform and improve the programme contents, structure, schedule and teaching for the following year.

The schools in the project adopted different approaches to evaluation. For example the Lithuanian school coordinator used group interviews and conversations to collect data from pupils. However, all the schools used open discussions in which children were free to express their opinions. Pupils' written and oral work was evaluated to find out whether pupils' learning met the prescribed outcomes of the project (see Section 3 in the Abstract). There was some inflexibility in the methods of evaluation used, as schools were limited by having to include evaluation methods laid out in the COMENIUS application.

Teams of teachers collected data in each school and shared results with their colleagues before these results were discussed at COMENIUS project meetings. No external evaluators were involved. The project outline and the schools involved drove the project's approach to evaluation. Its processes were participatory and democratic and its outcomes were open, self-determined and (co)created (see Figure 3.3). In Nummenpää this approach to evaluation was entirely consistent with the open and flexible approach of the Finnish Ministry of Education to self-evaluation in schools whereas in schools such as the Welsh school the open project approach to evaluation had to co-exist with a system of evaluation by inspection largely orchestrated by institutions and individuals outside the school.

Teachers' observations and open discussions were the main ways of evaluating a theme after it had been completed in Nummenpää School. Discussions took place in classes of around thirteen to fifteen pupils, which gave children and teachers time to listen to each other and discuss and share opinions.

However the school did design an innovative way of evaluating the work done in the first year of the project. Nummenpää School organised an outdoor trail as a less formal approach to evaluating the first year of the project. The children and their parents walked the trail, attempting the tasks located at stations along the trail. These tasks contained questions relating to the themes covered in the project's first year and questions about partner countries in the project. Teaching staff observed and assessed the children's and their parents' awareness and their ability to perform tasks such as sorting waste. The project coordinator conducted a short interview with the children and their parents at the end of the trail. Some of the questions she asked were:

- What was the best event in the project this year?
- Did you get enough information about the project?
- Shall we continue with the project next year?
- What are the benefits of the project?
- What are the negative effects of the project?

At the end of the second year a more conventional approach was taken to evaluation when teachers asked children for their opinions about the project. Teachers asked the children:

- Which was your favourite theme?
- Which event was the most remarkable for you?

126

- What would you like to change in the project?
- What has been difficult about the project?
- What are your ideas about the future development of the project?

At the end of the project members of the Parent's Committee who had been on the committee from the beginning to the end of the *Three Es project* were interviewed. They were asked:

- How had the project served its environmental aims?
- What were the benefits of the project?
- What criticisms did they have of the project?
- How did they feel the school's daily life had changed?
- What had impressed their children most during the three years of the project?

With these informal approaches to self-evaluation teaching staff did not feel it was necessary to organise official questionnaires or large-scale interviews.

Findings

EE is one of the main features of the formal curriculum of Nummenpää School. The teachers in the school are well trained in EE as a result of attending a number of national level continuing professional development (CPD) courses in EE. Teaching staff identified EE as a theme for development in the formal curriculum at Nummenpää School. The curriculum is based on common values shared by the school and the families of its pupils. These values emerged from discussions between parents and staff (Jääskeläinen and Nykänen, 1994).

The main internal driver for the development of the *Three Es project* was Nummenpää School's own curriculum and the school's commitment to sustainability values. A small announcement in a Finnish national teachers' journal, *Opettaja* ('teacher' in Finnish) advertising COMENIUS funding for CPD courses for teachers in European countries, started the process that led to the birth of the *Three Es project*. The teaching staff felt that EE could be developed further if one of the teachers attended a COMENIUS course in EE. Experience of an international EE course was thought to be the best option, as it would update EE knowledge in the school in an international setting. I successfully applied for a place on a COMENIUS course in EE.

My experiences on the COMENIUS professional development course *Creating a better environment in our school*, in the UK in 1999 were a major stimulus to the development of the *Three Es project*. This course gave teachers and other European educators a unique chance to update their knowledge of sustainability, environmental issues and EE/ESD. The course also trained course members to use materials from the *Sustainability Education in European Primary Schools* (SEEPS) Project to organise CPD programmes in EE/ESD in their own schools for their own staff (Shallcross, 2004). The SEEPS project places a heavy emphasis on whole school approaches to EE/ESD (see Chapter Eleven).

The three main values of the *Three Es project* were its emphasis on whole school development, learning by doing and networking. The following descriptions of each of these values underpinned the project:

- A whole school approach means that everyone is welcome and can be involved: everyone at school can do something and everyone's work is valuable.
- Learning by doing means that children's own active work for their environment is encouraged by aiming for the future by starting today. Adults act as role models by setting an example not just in talking about the environment but by doing things such as recycling at home, at school and in the community.
- Networking means that the schools kept local environmental authorities, communities and volunteers aware of the project: they involved them by consulting them and asking for help.

Adults and the school itself should model ESD (UNESCO, 2004) by giving children a positive example. This is not just EE/ESD being talked about in classrooms. The *Three Es project* is based on the belief that values are caught rather than taught, by schools and teachers practising what they teach. Thus the links between the formal and the non-formal curriculum become central to whole school development in EE/ESD. If schools advocate active citizenship, children and young people should be encouraged to participate in decision-making about actions in their schools and local communities. This not only makes children and young people aware of their responsibilities, but also increases their action competence (Mogensen, 1995) and their capacity to affect their environment. By empowering children and young people now this project should promote their development as active citizens in the future by illustrating that what they do now has real implications for the future (Hicks, 2001).

The European Commission (EC) Education Directorate funded the *Three Es project* as a COMENIUS school partnership for three years from 2000-2003. Nummenpää School was the coordinating school; the other six partner schools were from Lithuania, the Czech Republic, Wales, Cyprus and Italy. The main dimension of this project was to promote environmental work across the seven schools. The other two dimensions of international co-operation and ICT were designed to support this work and to motivate everyone who was involved. To save natural resources and to take care of natural heritage should be a planetary interest in which ICT can play a role by spreading information effectively, quickly and more sustainably than other forms of communication.

Each year of the three-year project was divided into two or three periods and each period had a theme focusing on a specified environmental issue. The first theme, the starting point for each year, was a focus on one of the re-sources maintaining life on Earth such as water (see Table 7.1) or air (University of Turku, 1997). Other themes covered during the project were recycling and re-using, waste, school surroundings, paper, energy, nutrition and trans-portation.

Multi-sensory approaches to learning were used to develop each pupil's own environmental sensitivity through direct experiences of nature. These ex-periences were intended to lead pupils to appreciate, understand and work for nature (van Matre, 1990). The project outcomes were many and varied:

- more sustainable ways of running institutional practices in each school such as sorting waste, saving water and promoting energy efficiency
- developing pleasanter school surroundings
- making contacts with local and regional environmental administrators
- publicising environmental issues in the media
- developing information and teaching materials about the project's themes
- increasing the motivation of teachers and children
- exposing teachers and pupils to new teaching methods

The project motivated children because learning became concrete as it dealt with real local issues (Uzzell et al, 1994; Jensen, 2002) and because other chil-dren in others countries were addressing the same EE themes. Other out-comes were the production of videos, CDs, articles, instruments, recipes, tapes, books and booklets. After each theme was finished, copies of materials were sent to each partner school. Nummenpää School organised two big public exhibitions of children's artwork that aimed to demonstrate the aesthetic value of the environment and nature (Kurttio, 1994). There was a permanent exhibition of project work at the school during the lifetime of the project. Materials were added to this exhibition after each theme. Work from the other six schools was also displayed. When parents evaluated the project, they said that the exhibitions were informative because they showed clearly what was going on and who had been involved.

Table 7.1: Outline of the teaching plan for the water theme at Nummenpää School

Concepts	Subjects integrated in the theme	Outdoor experiments	Indoor experiments	Fieldtrips
Water-cycle	Art	Investigating nearby ponds	Freezing and boiling water	Visit to a water purifying plant
Ecosystem	Finnish	Identifying aquatic plants	Evaporation	Visit to a swimming pool
Acid rain	English	Identifying aquatic animals	Surface tension	
Web of life	Science	pH testing		
	ICT/Internet			
	Sport			

There were some special highlights in this stimulating project. To keep up team morale and to remind everyone of the importance of environmental work, the schools organised some big events during the project:

1. The balloon happening, when balloons with slogans about air-protection were set free in each project country at the same moment. This event featured on national TV news in Cyprus.

2. The day without electricity; pupils and teachers studied by candlelight and made their lunch on a campfire when the temperature was minus 12°C in Paimio.

3. The day without cars, when walking, bicycles and public transport were shown to be alternatives to travelling by car. This event had to be organised in cooperation with the local police in each country.

The children were clearly most interested in the water theme, outdoor activities, first-hand experiences of nature with animals and/or plants and learning by doing. They learned, for example, that a pond is home for some organisms and homes need to be safe and protected. The parents' answers showed that they did not know very much about the project and that they needed more information. However the general opinion of both children and parents was very positive and encouraging; the only negative aspect that parents reported was that the teachers had so much extra work to do. In a staff meeting about the *Three Es project* teachers also complained that the project schedule was too busy.

When the outdoor trail was used as a stimulus for evaluation, the benefits of the project for the school's pupils which both children and their parents identified were:

- making new friends from different countries
- finding learning more interesting
- increased motivation and greater enthusiasm
- gaining new knowledge

The evaluation results from Nummenpää were shared and discussed with all the other partner schools in the project evaluation meeting. These formative evaluations were used to construct the educational plans for the next year of the project. If all or most of the schools identified the same problem, the project programme was changed. For example, at one meeting the project team decided to concentrate on three themes instead of four for the following year. However, the overwhelming perception of all the schools was that the project was successful. The project coordinator from Cyprus commented:

> The benefits of the *Three Es project* are plenty and numerous. Pupils were given opportunities to develop the skills and confidence necessary for active and effective community participation in the future. This was ensured through the active participation of the pupils in the whole project work, for instance they planned, researched, produced articles, drawings, constructions, reported to the partner schools, exchanged information, gave and got feedback.

The second year of the project had three themes: air, paper and energy and four happenings; a balloon happening, a children's art exhibition in the electricity museum, an art exhibition about nature and the day without electricity. All of these events were reported in the local or national media, partly because after the first year of the project the partners had decided that there was more work to do on public relations and bringing the project to public attention.

The children's views about the balloon happening and the day without electricity were positive. Pupils said that the art exhibitions were very rewarding for them, particularly when their work was valued and praised by visitors. However they thought that research work on the air theme was too theoretical. Despite their positive views about the day without electricity, pupils could not identify many ways of reducing electricity consumption in the school. This was disappointing.

The third year was a great challenge for Nummenpää as the final meeting of the *Three Es project* partners was held at the school. Parents' participation and active involvement in the project meant a lot to the school. Parents, along with children and staff, took part in cleaning the school's surroundings before the visit and parents looked after guests when they visited the exhibitions. The Parents' Committee made a big contribution to the *Three Es project*.

One ex-pupil of Nummenpää School identified the following benefits of being involved in the project.

> From my point of view environmental education is a very important part of a primary school's educational entity. Nature is such an important thing for me, therefore for example teachers' talking about recycling was information that I longed for and needed to get. Also an excursion to a windmill and studies of different sources of energy have been very educational. Those things (about nature and environment) we learned in the primary school have helped me to cope with secondary school work and will certainly affect my future in a positive way.

Other benefits of the project have been that the children's ICT skills have improved because they have been using the Internet, writing e-mails, plotting statistics and taking and editing photographs. Pupils were motivated because they used ICT for a real purpose to communicate with children in partner schools about the project. Computers have been useful tools for handling and delivering information, not for its own sake, but to address authentic local issues covered by the environmental themes addressed in the project. The prestige of the project meant that schools with less computer equipment were able to ask their local authority's school administration for more money to improve their ICT facilities, in order to cooperate more effectively with other schools in the project.

The project intended to make people more aware of their environmental and natural resources. The project has had a positive long-term effect on children's, parents' and staff attitudes toward EE partly because the publicity surrounding international cooperation has given environmental work a very bright halo at Nummenpää. This halo was seen in the pride pupils, parents and other stakeholders took in the project's work for environmental/sustainability issues. All of these people appeared to become committed to the common values that underpinned the project.

Whole school approaches involve not only teachers, children and parents but the rest of the school staff. The *Three Es project* influenced the school kitchen. The kitchen staff performed some sustainable catering practices before the T*hree Es project*, such as using locally produced foodstuffs whenever possible. When the theme was European food and nutrition, cooperation with the cook was both necessary and productive. The cook helped children with their cooking by obtaining recipes from partner schools, getting all the ingredients needed for recipes and cooking some of these recipes himself. When the school studied vegetarian food the cook demonstrated alternative vegetarian recipes to the pupils and teachers. When the electricity free day happened, the cook cooked on a campfire with the help of the children; this was one of the memorable highlights of the whole project. Although it was clearly not possible to improve everything about our food consumption, these and other experiences made us realise that we could re-use some food packaging and recycle others.

The school janitor's part in the project had one of the most long-lasting effects on the school' s everyday life. The janitor took an active role in environmental issues and education because she is a very committed environmentalist who supports sustainable values. All the cleaning and polishing liquids used in the school are environmentally friendly. The janitor oversees the use of paper-towels and water, the recycling and sorting of waste (paper, glass, metal, organic) and the tidiness of schoolrooms. She volunteered to wash fabric towels so that children did not have to use paper towels.

The janitor also monitors the wasteful use of electricity in the school and it was she who suggested that the school should participate in the local environmental association's sustainability competition, which was really worthwhile because the school was awarded a prize! The public recognition of Nummenpää School's progress in sustainability work has been very encouraging. In 2002 the Paimio Local Agenda 21 Committee gave its annual prize to Nummenpää School. The diploma that came with this award referred to Nummenpää School as an example of an institution doing very good environmental and sustainability work.

However, the international cooperation that led to some of these benefits for Nummenpää School does raise some problems. School systems differ in

European countries. In some cases national curricula requirements for project work, inspections, annual exams or strict guidelines affecting subjects had to be considered at project planning meetings. The flexible Finnish national curriculum meant that Nummenpää School could easily incorporate the three themes of air water and earth into its curriculum planning. However, the small size of the school made it difficult for the teaching staff to cover all the activities in these themes.

Another problem with EC projects is the bureaucracy surrounding funding. COMENIUS funding was crucial for the *Three Es project*. Unfortunately, it took great efforts by the partners to complete the application for the renewal of funding because the deadline for applications fell in the middle of the project year. Another problem was that the project evaluation was not ready in time for the next bid to be submitted, so the COMENIUS schedule did not fit the project schedule. But these problems could be solved.

Conclusion: Minus 18 degrees and we're still going strong!
(Extract from a Nummenpää School report)

> The main difference is in the level of honest self-appraisal needed to ensure that the adults participate with the children and don't simply impose their own worn-out agendas in the old worn-out way. This work makes the same demands on the parents as it does on the children. It is nothing less than trans-generational, joint effort, the same effort made from different starting-points. It is a shared adventure. (Farrer with Hawkes, 2000: 142)

The network started and continued largely because of enthusiastic individuals; team spirit and goodwill created by the project encouraged and motivated people. As some pupils from the Czech Republic wrote in a summary letter: 'we realised that what's done for nature today is done for our future'. This comment shows that this project has helped children to see the connections between the health of natural and socio-economic systems as well as educating them as future planetary citizens (Hicks, 2001).

Initially the project was not intended to be a model for EE but it produced more EE materials than expected. The transferability of these materials and ideas could have been much wider if the results of the project had been externally evaluated. It would have been touching if ICT had promoted more personal contact, from one child to another, but the limited ICT resources and skills in the schools did not make this feasible.

International and national cooperation and development work is extremely important in EE/ESD to address environmental issues and sustainability. In some schools in the project EE/ESD work had to be supported by funding from a European authority, in this case COMENIUS, before it got support from the local authorities. Many institutions are doing excellent work in raising their standards of sustainability but they could reach even higher standards by networking. Isolation inside or between institutions kills enthusiasm slowly but surely.

Teacher education is important. Five of the six partner countries in the *Three Es project* were linked in one way or another to the COMENIUS course run in the UK in 1999. This course not only provided information but made international contacts available. The course made participants aware of what was needed for a successful international cooperation project.

Teachers live their everyday lives in schools as role models (Coles, 1997) who affect children's and young people's attitudes and actions. Through professional development courses and other CPD experiences teachers can share the contextual knowledge gained from their own school's experiences with other teachers. This sharing of contextual knowledge is highly valued by other educational professionals. But international cooperation is a question of money as well as values. Do national governments and the European Union see the investment in EE/ESD for teachers as worthwhile or will it continue to be marginalised despite the advent of the UN decade of ESD (2005-2014)?

8

Redeveloping a school's physical environment

Konstandina Tamoutseli with Paul Pace

Introduction

This chapter describes how a primary school in Greece made significant changes to its physical environment, both inside and outside the school buildings, through two collaborative and participatory EE[10] projects: *Our school grounds are our world* and *Using nature and art to improve the school environment*. These projects fostered strong links with the local community, developed pupils' self-esteem and helped to promote more discursive, cooperative learning in the school. In order to participate in designing change, some pupils became researchers. As a result of these projects the school's redevelopment plans have become a model for changing schools in the local area.

Abstract

1. Description of the School
Second Primary School of Sykies, Thessaloniki, Greece has 24 teachers and 340 pupils, both boys and girls aged from six to twelve years old. It is situated in the rather poor, densely built-up urban area of Sykies, a municipality in the west of Thessaloniki. All the school's pupils come from the immediate locality.

2. Aims and Outcomes of the Project
The aim of the two EE projects was to create attractive and open learning environments both inside the school and in its grounds. The objectives were to:

- encourage pupils to cooperate and work in groups
- redevelop classroom environments

- use the school grounds as a teaching resource
- improve the aesthetic and functional quality of the classrooms and the school grounds and make the grounds safer
- promote children's awareness and care for the school and local environment by creating opportunities for them to participate in the redevelopment process
- enhance children's creativity, problem-solving and research skills and in particular their ability to collect, analyse and present data
- create an appealing outdoor environment which could serve as a model of alternative design for the use of outdoor space for the local community

3. The Project: Content and Development
The school initiated two projects: *Our school grounds are our world* and *Using nature and art to improve the school environment*. There was a focus on the school's physical environment because this was rather harsh and did not stimulate learning. Two fourth and fifth grade teachers with classes of pupils aged ten and eleven, with the support of other teachers, collaborated with their pupils to improve the school's physical environment so that this could be used as an educational resource. The projects were interdisciplinary and connected to various curriculum subjects such as Language, Mathematics, Science and Art.

4. Drivers: a) External b) Internal
a) The EE advisor for the area organised seminars for primary school teachers and headteachers on the development of the school's physical environment.

b) The two teachers who ran the EE projects wanted to create attractive open learning environments inside and outside the school buildings to support cooperative methods of learning and raise children's environmental awareness by increasing their interest, first for the immediate environment and then for the local and global environment.

5. Assessment
From the experience of working together in the project, children developed social skills and also skills in Language, Mathematics, Design, Art, Biological Sciences, and New Technologies. Pupils were assessed on their ability to learn how to process text, locate and highlight important information, make summaries and develop Powerpoint presentations.

6. Evaluation
According to the teachers the appealing and friendly environment created by the project is greatly appreciated by pupils and has increased their interest in learning and their level of participation in class. It has introduced new learning and teaching approaches, such as experiential and cooperative learning. These approaches address Greek National Curriculum targets. The projects have introduced the local community to innovative and participatory approaches to school and community development.

7. Constraints or Difficulties in Developing the Project
Completing the whole school redevelopment plan will take some time, so it is possible that some of the children who participated in the project will leave the school before the project is completed. The two projects only engaged about 20 per cent of the school's teaching staff so ways need to be found to involve more school staff.

8. Benefits of the Project

The participative approach to the project:

- led to the whole school community cooperating in achieving a common goal
- helped pupils to develop skills in communication, negotiation, teamwork and community involvement
- raised the interest of local government authorities and many other schools in the area in adopting a participatory approach to developing school environments
- emphasised the link between the school's physical environment and teaching approaches and the need to improve both

9. Future Developments

- promoting further school development plans for the indoor and outdoor environment
- developing an in-service teacher training course in the use of cooperative and holistic methods of teaching and learning to develop school grounds as an educational resource

Research

The three aims of the research at the Second Primary Schools of Sykies were to identify:

- benefits of the EE projects for the school and its local community
- features of the school's culture and ethos which promote the development of EE
- barriers to the implementation of EE in the school

The research used a pluralist, partly self-evaluative approach which was ethnographic in that it concentrated on observation of the school community and wherever possible involved members of this community (Woods, 1996) in the collection of data about whole school approaches. This model was pluralist because it drew on both qualitative and quantitative data and on research methodologies such as ethnography that are rooted in the belief that knowledge is socially constructed. However when environmental improvement is investigated there is room for empirical research such as the increase in the number of plants in the school's grounds. Researching the social construction of knowledge implies research instruments such as individual and group interviews or open-ended semi-structured questionnaires, whereas collecting factual data about the environment involves more quantitative methods such as audits and surveys (see Chapter Five). Data of both types were collected for this research.

Before the research began the lead researcher visited the school to seek the headteacher's approval and to discuss the purposes and methods of the research. The headteacher subsequently discussed the research with all members of the teaching staff and obtained their consent for it to proceed. As the lead researcher was the EE advisor for the area she knew about the EE projects being implemented in the school because she had already collaborated with teachers on the development of teaching methodologies and support materials. She was not just an observer of the process that led to the development of the EE project in the school: she was both participant and observer, what Gold (1958) calls a participant-as-observer.

The headteacher's and the teachers' attitudes towards EE and whole school approaches were investigated using a questionnaire and interviews. The questionnaire was piloted with the headteacher and the EE teachers in the school during the lead researcher's first visit. Collaboration with this group of EE teachers and the headteacher resulted from a long-standing association with the lead researcher. During a second visit, the lead researcher handed out a copy of the questionnaire to all the teachers individually, along with the instructions necessary to complete it. These questionnaires (see Appendix 8.1) sought to investigate what teachers thought the differences were between how they felt EE should be addressed in the school and how it was actually practised.

The teachers were given a week to complete the questionnaire, which asked them to rank from one to six the statements about EE which best reflected EE practice in their school. They were then asked to rank the same statements to identify the six statements that best described what EE should be like in their school. There were questions about in-service training that explored how and by whom in-service training should be provided. They were also asked to rank those sources of in-service training they considered relevant to their school from a list given in the questionnaire. The last section of the questionnaire asked teachers to classify 24 suggested topics for in-service training in EE for their school, in order of importance, from a list given in the questionnaire. The questionnaire also included questions about the school's environmental policy and action plan.

After returning the questionnaires, all the participating teachers were interviewed in groups of five, apart from the headteacher and the EE teachers who were interviewed individually. The headteacher and the EE teachers were willing to be interviewed individually because of their previous collaboration with the lead researcher in working together on other EE projects. The rest of the teachers wanted to be interviewed in groups as this made them feel more relaxed and confident and because they wanted to hear each others' opinions. The interviews examined how teachers promoted social and environmental change in their school. These interviews tried to distinguish between teachers' roles as classroom practitioners and as members of a school community. The classification suggested in Table 5.3 was used to analyse the attitude of teachers to social and environmental change.

A sample of 10 per cent of the fourth and fifth grade pupils, boys and girls aged eleven or twelve, were interviewed in pairs to investigate their perceptions of the school's social organisation, its degree of pupil participation in decision-making and its culture and ethos. These same points were addressed in interviews with teachers. All the pupils interviewed had participated in the EE projects that had rejuvenated their classrooms or school grounds. The purpose of interviewing pupils was not just to discover what their views of their school were, but also to cross-reference or triangulate with the views of teachers. Hart's (1997) classification of levels of children participation (see Table 2.1) was used to analyse and compare child and adult responses. The highest and lowest levels of child participation were decided on the basis of the comments teachers and pupils made during these interviews about curriculum, positive changes in the local community and institutional practices in the school, especially the development of school grounds and the redevelopment of classroom environments.

To produce proposals for the redevelopment of their classrooms and their school's grounds pupils worked with action research methods under the guidance of their two teachers. These methods combined methodological tools from Psychology, Architecture, Education and Social Psychology. The pupil researchers collected data about other pupils' feelings about characteristics of the classrooms and the school grounds (positive-negative, liked-disliked) and behavioural problems resulting from children's negative perceptions of the school's physical environment.

They also developed a questionnaire that was addressed to all the pupils in the school and was also distributed to parents and school staff. This questionnaire explored how pupils wanted to use their school grounds, and the educational features they would like to see in the grounds, and the ways in which parents and school staff thought that the school's grounds could be used. All the data were analysed, processed and used to prepare the final proposal for a redevelopment plan for the school's physical environment.

Findings

The questionnaires were analysed both statistically and qualitatively. The evidence showed that teachers thought that current EE practice permeated all subjects, was concerned with the active involvement of pupils in improving and caring for their classrooms and school grounds and raised awareness of the main global environmental issues such as acid rain and global warming. The teachers also thought that EE was relevant to all subjects and taught by all teachers, that it involved the active participation of pupils in improving the school environment, learning about their local environment through fieldwork and investigation, and developed understanding of the local and global impact of decisions on the environment.

The analysis of what EE should be like in primary schools revealed little difference between this and how they thought EE was working in their school. However they stressed that EE should develop positive attitudes to the environment through discussion and should promote pupils' active involvement in improving their environment. These two views are important in understanding the focus of the two EE projects at the Second Primary School of Sykies and their concern with active group and cooperative learning.

The majority of teachers wanted more in-service training on running EE projects in school. The responses to the questionnaires showed that the teachers wanted training methods that included, in order of priority:

- school-based training led by external trainers
- conferences or seminars
- part-time time certified or non-certified distance learning courses, including the use of the Internet

Their in-service training needs were, in order of priority:

- values education
- research or evaluation of school environmental practices
- philosophical perspectives on EE
- development and sustainability
- self-evaluation strategies for EE in schools
- pupil participation in decision-making about EE
- developing school grounds

There is a clear association between these two sets of priorities and the content and focus of the two EE projects. The teachers pointed out that their school lacked an environmental policy, an environmental action plan and an EE coordinator. The majority agreed that these deficiencies should be addressed urgently in the school's development plans. Statistical analysis of the questionnaires and evaluation of the interview data showed that the school had assets which could be used for the development of the two EE projects.

The main asset was the positive attitude of a number of teachers towards new teaching approaches, such as group and cooperative learning and whole language teaching. These teachers were also willing to act as agents of change in the school. A second asset was the good relationship between teachers and the Parent Council, which is very supportive of initiatives in the school. Teachers were also supportive of children's participation in decision-making, at least in the EE projects. They were also open-minded about extra-curricular activities and in-service training. The teacher's positive attitude towards training is significant, as teachers' performance is not evaluated in Greek schools. The school has an open attitude to the local community and values the improvement of the school's physical and educational environment. All these assets helped the school to start to develop a whole school approach to EE.

Unfortunately, despite these positive responses only about 20 per cent of teachers are involved in EE projects in the school. These teachers were affective or active teachers (see Table 5.2), who used specific teaching strategies to develop social or environmental action directly concerned with environmental change in the school and its grounds. Eighty per cent of teachers only got involved in social and environmental change when issues of personal interest arose. The reason given by these teachers for their limited involvement in EE was that it is an extra-curricular activity which they had no time to deal with.

Interviews were conducted after the questionnaires had been analysed. When asked if they thought that education changed attitudes all the teachers said that there was a direct relationship between education and attitudinal change in pupils. For example teacher one said: 'Of course, through teaching and the teacher's own example, especially through experiences.' Teacher two's response was similar: 'Of course, through experiences and children-children and teacher-children interactions.' Teachers thought that the main factors influencing attitude change were teacher behaviour, activities organised in school and children's interactions with each other. This view, though not surprising, perhaps overemphasises the role of the formal curriculum in promoting attitudinal change and downplays the impact of the non-formal curriculum (see Chapter Two).

The teachers all agreed that cooperation was needed in the school community and that change should take place in the school through the 'involvement of the whole school community' (Teacher three). All the teachers agreed that the school could influence local communities by 'undertaking actions personally and empowering others to work with each other' (Teacher four). This whole school-community involvement was achieved at various stages in the *Using nature and art to improve the school environment* project. The community was involved in fundraising at the Christmas bazaar, at a barbeque and on the project presentation days. When pupils were asked the same question about whether school could influence their local community they said:

> Pupil one: Of course, it can. For example, it can influence them through influencing parents and through the function of the school itself, which can serve as a paradigm[11].

> Pupil two: Yes, by opening up the school activities to the local community, as well as through collaborations, and with the school paradigm itself.

All the teachers considered it vital for social and environmental practices to be applied in school and the local community and they wanted to see more initiatives from the school. They felt that the use of their school grounds as an educational resource was restricted because currently the grounds had no educational value. Although 90 per cent of the teachers said that environmental issues were taught through all the subjects, only 20 per cent acknowledged working on EE projects themselves. Eighty per cent of the teachers valued participatory approaches to action as the best ways of influencing communities, while 20 per cent considered that this influence could be achieved through parents and role modelling by the school.

Some discussion sessions encouraged pupils to express their opinions about their level of participation in decision-making, about affairs in their own class and about whole school matters. Pupils described a profound difference in their levels of participation in these areas. With the exception of EE projects, they felt they were not encouraged to participate in making decisions about whole school issues:

> Pupil three: Concerning issues related to our class, we participate but this mainly depends on the teacher. In school matters, decisions are taken elsewhere and they just ask us in the end whether we agree or not. In EE programmes, they listen to us.

Pupil four: For class related matters the students' opinions are considered but in matters related to the whole school, in general, they rarely take our views into consideration. Only through EE programmes are our views on general school matters respected.

The two EE projects seem to have had a major effect in improving pupils' opinions about their participation in whole school affairs. But when it came to the extent of pupils' participation in decisions about the nature and content of learning, all the pupils who were interviewed agreed that this depended entirely upon the class teacher. The school did not have a policy on pupil participation in decisions about teaching and learning. The teachers all agreed that there were differences in pupil participation between subject areas and classes, again depending on the teacher, but they agreed that levels of participation increased as pupils grew older.

The prospect of sharing more power and responsibility for decision-making with pupils about institutional practice and curriculum was not encouraging, because of the highly centralised Greek educational system. Pupils only got involved in changes affecting the local community when the community requested their participation. This mostly happened in the EE projects. Overall there was also a slight difference in levels of pupil participation, ranging from non-participation to low levels of participation across the three areas of curriculum, institutional practice and community involvement, again with the exception of those pupils involved in the EE projects (see Table 2.1).

There is a school council consisting of teachers, parents and representatives of the local authorities but it is not very active. Parents and representatives of the local authorities are elected while the headmaster represents the school. Pupils are not represented on this council because the headteacher and teachers thought they were too young to be involved. Pupils generally believed that they were not trusted because of their age: 'They consider us too young to know the right thing but this is not true' (Pupil five). 'I haven't thought about it but I think it is the age' (Pupil six). This seems to show that most teachers see children as citizens in waiting rather than currently active citizens – an ideology that does not consider children equipped to participate in the process of change (Alderson, 2000). It would be interesting to know what stance the EE teachers took on this issue.

However, pupils are sometimes asked to participate in school staff meetings if this is appropriate to the topic being discussed. Interviews with pupils who participated in the EE projects have been cross-referenced with teachers' views about pupil participation. It appears from both sets of interviews that pupils' opinions were taken into consideration in a variety of situations and the degree of their participation depended on individual teacher's attitudes and their preferred teaching approaches.

When pupils did participate outside the context of their own classes, this was mainly in community-focused projects outside school, except for the two EE projects. Pupils claimed high levels of participation in EE projects (see Table 2.1), in which although adults initiated ideas, pupils are actively involved in making decisions about the development of these ideas. As for the rest of school life, pupils' participation appears to be purely tokenist. For example, there is a class council elected by class members but it has a limited jurisdiction.

The teachers mostly agreed that there was a broadly collaborative school culture in which leadership allowed major decisions about change to be taken democratically; all members of the teaching staff vote on decisions and the majority view is adopted. However some administrative decisions are made by the headteacher alone. So although there is a participatory form of democracy, membership is restricted to teaching staff. On the other hand, 75 per cent of teachers thought that they could try to influence change in school through cooperation with the parents' council, while 20 per cent emphasised the need to involve the headteacher in change, through EE projects, and 5 per cent saw a need to change the headteacher's role.

When teachers were asked to identify environmentally and socially friendly practices in the school, 20 per cent mentioned control over the quality of food served in the school refectory and meetings of teaching staff with the parents' council and representatives from the local authorities. As far as food is concerned, the amount of junk food sold in the school is limited, while healthy foods such as milk and fresh fruit juices, traditional *koulouri* (Greek bread with sesame) and cheese pies made freshly every day, are promoted. There was unanimous agreement that the school's main development target should be the improvement of the school's physical and social environment. The teachers felt that if this was achieved, the school could serve as a cultural centre for the neighbourhood. All the teachers considered the relationship between the school and the local community to be good and democratic. Overall they felt that the school had an equal share of organic and mechanistic features (see Table 5.4). For example that communication and policy change and initiation were broadly organic, whereas structure and control were mechanistic.

Ninety five per cent of the teachers considered the leadership style in the school to be democratic and only 5 per cent considered it political-authoritarian (see Table 5.5). These were the same teachers who saw a need for the headteacher's role to become more democratic in order to raise the school's participation in EE projects. Although the headteacher positively supports these projects, this support is not the main internal driving force for the implementation of whole school approaches in the school: the enthusiasm of a minority of highly motivated teachers is more important. Of course the headteacher's support is of great value in maintaining the dynamism and stamina of this small group of teachers.

The projects
The architecture of the Second Primary School of Sykies was not very child-friendly. It consists of three-storey buildings set in very restricted and steep grounds. This means that movement between indoors and outdoors and within the buildings created health and safety risks. The school's physical environment also lacked stimuli to motivate and promote learning. The classrooms lacked warmth and were not arranged in ways that supported cooperative methods of teaching and learning. The grounds were entirely covered by asphalt, conveying the impression that the school did not care about nature or the welfare of many of its pupils. Although parts of the grounds were marked out for basketball, there was no vegetation nor any educational or play facilities. To make things worse, the town of Sykies also lacks open spaces for safe outdoor play.

However, the school has a rich educational life and is open to extra-curricular activities. Local authorities are very helpful in funding these activities, mainly the EE projects. Most of the school staff live in the neighbourhood and support the transformation of the school into a cultural centre, which will be open to the community, have rich and varied functions and an attractive physical environment. But cultural and environmental change in schools is not easy in the highly centralised Greek educational system, which is tightly structured and test-driven. For example because the uniform national curriculum for all primary schools in Greece is taught using standard textbooks this can discourage local school-focused curricular initiatives. Although the Greek system gives teachers the freedom to decide teaching approaches, teaching still remains quite teacher-led and lecture based in many schools (Noutsos, 1983: Bouzakis, 2000).

Despite these difficulties, two fourth and fifth grade teachers, the physical education teacher and the teachers of art and new technologies collaborated on two EE projects which set out to transform the school's physical environment and to promote more cooperative and group learning. To develop these projects the school used a participatory approach to EE involving school staff, pupils, parents, experts, members of local authorities and art students. The titles of the environmental projects were *Our school grounds are our world* and *Using nature and art to improve the school environment.* These projects were not just school based; they were connected with the community outside the school.

In the *Using nature and art to improve the school environment* project, teachers from many subject areas have cooperated with and been supported by parents and local authorities. Experts in fields related to the two EE projects, such as architects, landscape architects and educationalists from the private sector were invited into the school and field trips were conducted for the pupils in the local community. Financial support for the projects came from local authorities but the school also raised funds itself. A Christmas bazaar was organised that not only helped to raise money but also publicised the projects more widely and promoted community involvement.

Through this project, classrooms were painted in bright colours. New whiteboards replaced old chalkboards. A seated area with a carpet, sofas and a table was created in the corner of each classroom for group gatherings, discussions, resting and reading. Classrooms were also decorated with pupils' paintings, plants and small aquaria. Each class had a library created from books brought into school by children. The corridors were furnished with wooden tables and benches and decorated with plants.

Two CD-Roms were produced. The first describes the process behind the classroom redevelopment project and includes interactive activities about indoor and outdoor plants used in the project, as well as interactive games such as crosswords and hangman. The second refers to *Our school grounds are our world.* Both were distributed to the teaching staff, the Mayor of the Municipality of Sykies, members of the school council and all the pupils who had participated in the projects. A school library was founded using 100 books the children won in a story writing competition and money raised by the parents' council. A computer room was developed which was used to prepare the CD-Roms about the two EE projects.

In the second project, children were involved with the redevelopment of the school's central courtyard, which is an atrium surrounded by classrooms. They planted a variety of plants in the courtyard and helped to prune existing ones. Pupils also painted the courtyard walls in bright colours and decorated them with murals of plants and birds. The redevelopment plan for the grounds included work such as painting and decorating the concrete fence around the courtyard, planting annual and perennial plants and bushes in level garden beds created in the courtyard, filling planters with herbs and putting wooden benches in the grounds. Art students from the local university worked with children on their preliminary designs for the school grounds in class and on implementing them in the grounds. The project was publicised in the local community by putting up posters of children's paintings in the streets. A professional artist worked with children to help them to calculate the volume of each colour of paint needed to paint the walls. The local authority sent workers to help prepare and finish off the surfaces of these walls. When the painting was finished, a festive day and barbeque was organised for the art students and children who had spent two days decorating the walls. Parents brought the food.

Local authorities were impressed by the work done by the school and invited experts from the private sector and from the local university to construct a redevelopment plan for the whole school, in cooperation with the school community. The proposal for the redevelopment of the physical environment of the whole school was finalised after repeated discussions and presentations of plans by experts, local authorities, children and school staff. The plan is designed to create aesthetically appealing, stimulating and flexible indoor and outdoor teaching environments. The experts spent a day presenting the final plans for the project to the pupils at the school. On a separate occasion the plan was presented to the local community. The plan was also included in the school's newsletter, which is distributed to parents and local authorities. After a series of discussions among children and staff, this plan was presented to the whole school and accepted. This project is fully funded by the local authorities and will be used as a model for the redevelopment of the rest of the schools in the Sykies area.

With the cooperation of experts the redevelopment plans will use research to transform knowledge of school environments by applying pedagogical, psychosocial and architectural research criteria and methods (Tamoutseli, 1999). These methods included observing pupil behaviour in relation to specific characteristics of spaces, oral and graphic interviews about spatial preferences, interviews about spatial perception and evaluations of the safety and the aesthetic characteristics of spaces.

As part of this project the experts led in-service seminars for the teachers. These seminars explored the educational value and impact of the non-formal curriculum, the impact of the school's physical environment, especially its buildings and grounds, on the learning of pupils. Some of the teachers also attended in-service training on cooperative teaching and learning and whole school approaches. These seminars presented a contrast to the teacher-oriented educational model, with its emphasis on cognitive development, that is still the main focus of the Greek educational system (Germanos, 2002). As a result of these seminars and their own experiences several teachers in the school were convinced of the links between the pedagogical and psychosocial needs of their pupils and the need to develop the school's grounds and buildings as one way of meeting these needs.

The two EE projects *Our school grounds are our world* and *Using nature and art to improve the school environment* have raised children's self-esteem and sense of citizenship by allowing them to contribute their own ideas to the redevelopment of their school's indoor and outdoor spaces. The school staff, parents and local authorities involved in the two projects also demonstrated increased citizenship values: these adults, through their own personal efforts and financial assistance helped to implement the redevelopment proposals developed by the pupils. They also participated in meetings at which the experts' redevelopment plans were discussed, contributed their ideas to the formulation of these plans and helped with the care and management of the school's physical environment.

The benefits of the EE projects were that:

- the whole school community was engaged in a common project
- the school formed links with and opened up to the local community as well as to local authorities
- because children had participated in the projects they were able to appreciate the processes of environmental design and the human role in these processes
- by creating flexible micro-environments inside school and in its grounds, teachers were able to reduce teacher-oriented methods and support cooperative, participatory methods of teaching and learning

Conclusion

Research findings supported the view that in the Second Primary School of Sykies school:

- EE projects on issues of direct interest to pupils and teachers, such as the school's physical environment, help pupils to engage in their own learning. Children are encouraged, through their own interest and active participation, to shape their immediate environment and to develop practices that correspond with sustainable practices in society at large

- the EE projects motivated local authorities to become involved in a school-initiated project

- parents from the local community were keen to participate in the EE projects. They were interviewed about and involved in the redevelopment work and in discussions with designers about the redevelopment plan. They were also invited to the Christmas bazaar and to the final presentation day about the projects

This case study demonstrates that no matter how highly centralised the educational system, as it is in Greece, motivated teachers can find ways of implementing new teaching approaches and establishing connections with their local community and with local authorities. Although national policy for the implementation of EE in Greece regards EE as an optional extra-curricular activity (Ministry of Education, 1991), the policy still suggests that whole school approaches should be introduced into primary education. However, this study shows that there is often a dislocation between the positive attitudes of teachers towards EE and their implementation of it.

The teachers at the Second Primary School of Sykies recognised the need to improve the physical and social environment in their school and acknowledged that EE projects were a means to this end. Yet there was still a low level of teacher involvement in these projects. Even though the school is closing the gap between knowledge, values and actions in EE, this research shows that this gap still limits the involvement of the majority of teachers. In-service training could be the answer. Structured school-focused courses would empower less motivated teachers to develop EE projects by dissolving some of the attitudinal and skills barriers to the implementation of whole school approaches to EE. This solution is examined in Chapter Eleven.

Acknowledgement

The authors would like to thank the EE teachers at the Second Primary School of Sykies, Maria Papadopoulou and Evangelia Tympa, for their constructive cooperation in the research, the head teacher for being so helpful and all the teachers in the school for participating in the research.

Appendix 8.1

1. Questionnaire on EE in your school

1.1: Below is a table with ten statements about EE. In column A, rank in order of importance from one to six, the statements which best reflect EE practice in your school. In column B, rank from one to six the statements which best describe what you think EE should be like in primary schools. You may rank all ten if you wish.

A	Statement	B
	1. EE is part of the school programme only as an extra-curricular activity or as an environment week.	
	2. EE means learning about environmental problems such as acid rain and global warming.	
	3. EE is a subject like maths and should only be taught by specialist EE teachers.	
	4. EE is relevant to all subjects and is taught by all teachers.	
	5. EE is mainly ecology; the study of plants and animals, their habitats and inter-relationships.	
	6 EE is about schools practising what they teach by fostering environmental responsibility in pupils, teachers and support staff.	
	7. EE is about developing positive attitudes towards the environment in pupils through the discussion of opinions and values education.	
	8. EE is concerned with the active involvement of pupils in improving the school environment.	
	9. EE involves pupils learning about their local environment through fieldwork and investigation.	
	10. EE is about understanding the local and global impact of our decisions on the environment.	

9

We can all make a difference: The Green Club and one teacher's determination

Paul Pace

Introduction

This study illustrates how one dedicated teacher in a Maltese school made a difference in her school by gaining the support of the headteacher, teachers, pupils, support staff and parents. It reinforces the point made in Chapter Eight that headteacher support is not necessarily the main internal driving force behind successful EE or ESD[12] projects. The study also shows that an EE project can succeed in a large, highly academic secondary school that has a strong drive to improve pupils' attainment. One significant question is whether such projects contribute to increased academic attainment by pupils, individually and collectively. This case study demonstrates that success is much more likely if the agent of change, in this case the coordinating teacher, targets initiatives at win/win situations by understanding and working with the academic ideology that drives the school (see Chapter Four).

Abstract

1. The School: St Theresa's Girls Junior Lyceum
a state secondary school in Malta, with a population of 1050 students aged eleven to sixteen.

2. Aims and Outcomes of the Project
The Green Club aims to:

- promote awareness and knowledge about the Maltese environment with special emphasis on the natural environment
- enhance biodiversity in the school grounds
- develop an awareness of the environmental impact of human activity
- promote sustainable practices among students and their parents

3. The Project: Content and Development
Since its inception in 1990, the club meets regularly to discuss environmental issues relevant to the school, identified by the coordinating teacher and pupils and ways in which these issues can be addressed. Activities can be grouped under two major categories:

1. those aimed at raising the environmental awareness of the general school population, for example club members address their peers during assemblies to encourage their participation in club activities and to provide information about environmental issues
2. those aimed at improving the school environment. For example, the club created a nature patch within the school grounds and planted indigenous trees that are cared for by club members

4. Drivers: a) External b) Internal
(a) The Green Club is not linked to any external project. Although the club is sometimes supported by BirdLife Malta, its development does not involve any external partner.

(b) The project originated from the enthusiasm of an English language teacher, an active BirdLife Malta member, who wanted to help pupils to develop an environmental ethic that would help them take concrete actions to protect their environment. The initiative is primarily an internal concern and all decisions are taken internally.

5. Assessment
No formal summative or formative assessment is carried out in the club. However, classes are given prizes for their achievements in the annual *Green Your Classroom Award*. The school also awards prizes for club initiatives at the school's annual prize day.

6. Evaluation
Although no structured evaluation is carried out, towards the end of each term the teachers in charge of the club and its pupil members meet to review the club's activities and their impact. Success is judged by whether objectives have been reached.

7. Constraints or Difficulties in Developing the Project
Although lack of funds is a limiting factor, finding enough time is the major problem for the club. Coordinating the club is an additional burden for teachers with other school responsibilities. Preparation for examinations also hinders pupil participation. Since the club's activities run during pupils' free time, the coordinator considers formal evaluation an added burden with the limited time available.

8. Benefits of the Project
The club's actions have improved the school grounds and the pupils' level of environmental awareness. Pupils who have been active club members tend to become active members of environmental non-governmental organisation (NGOs) such as BirdLife Malta.

9. Future Developments
There are plans to share the club's experiences with other Maltese schools with the aim of setting up a school environmental network in Malta. Opportunities to extend the Green Club initiative to European schools through twinning programmes are being explored.

Research

The aim of this research study was to gather data from the various stakeholders in the school community to build a case study that represents as accurately as possible the characteristic features of the initiative. For this purpose data was gathered over two academic years, mainly through semi-structured individual interviews, with the headteacher, two teachers who are not directly involved in the Green Club, two pupil members of the Green Club, the coordinating teacher, who was interviewed twice and a group interview with five pupils who are not Green Club members.

Most of the interviews took place during informal sessions and were aimed at triangulating or cross-checking the data gathered. The variety of perspectives of the interviewees allowed the researcher to collect various snapshots of school reality that made the case study report more coherent and as authentic a representation of school life as possible.

Being a parent representative on the School Council, I had access to circulars from the Maltese education authorities, school reports and the School Development Plan (SDP). These official documents provide important information about the policies that underpin any activity occurring in the school. The review and contextual analysis of these official documents gave me insight into the factors affecting the implementation of the initiative.

Findings
Formal curriculum and pedagogy

The Maltese educational system is highly selective, with selection starting early, when pupils are eight years old. Examinations play a critical role in determining progress since they control pupils' access to opportunities to further their education. Access to St Theresa's Junior Lyceum is controlled by selective examinations at the end of primary school. Consequently, the predominant pedagogy adopted is examination-oriented characterised by traditional, transmissional, stereotyped teaching styles and overloaded syllabuses (Pace, 1997a). This is particularly true of a Junior Lyceum, where students are expected to excel in their studies. Nevertheless, there has been a gradual and sustained effort, both from the Maltese educational authorities and from teachers, for a widening of the educational experience and the latest National Minimum Curriculum (NMC) illustrates this shift of emphasis in educational policy (Ministry of Education, 1999).

EE is still not mandatory in the NMC. To date there is no formal policy that provides guidelines for EE. EE in schools is either incidental or covered by extracurricular activities. Although several official reports give the impression that EE is being addressed in the curriculum, they refer only to the increase in the number of environmental topics in subject syllabuses after the setting up of the local Matriculation and Secondary Education Certificate (MATSEC) Examinations Board in 1992 (Pace, 1997a).

It is no wonder that all the teachers interviewed cited 'the lack of time available' as the principal problem they encounter in trying to develop school-based EE. In this context, schools/teachers wishing to include EE in their practice need to resort to other means. The Green Club's activities are mainly carried out during morning assemblies and lunch breaks and are not related to any particular curriculum subject. The club regularly organises photographic competitions and exhibitions.

> In a school like ours, academic achievement gets top priority. One cannot expect students to regularly miss out on lessons ... even though it's for a good cause. I would personally object to this. That is one of the reasons why the club's activities are carried out during breaks and during assemblies. (Co-ordinating teacher)

The role played by the coordinating teacher in promoting environmental or social change appears to lie somewhere between the active and the integrated levels (Table 5.3). While she considers environmental and social change as central to her teaching, she makes full use of institutional and curricular structures and a high level of democratic pupil participation to achieve her goals (see Table 2.1). Her colleagues tend to operate mainly at the cognitive level, believing that environmental and social action follows from environmental awareness. However, some teachers adopt an affective role (Table 5.3) because they feel that their teaching should include learning moments that focus on the development of attitudes and values:

> Our school believes a lot in the educational value of morning assemblies ... They are viewed as an opportunity to communicate certain important aspects that we might find difficult to deal with in class because of the over-crowded syllabus ... the environment is one such subject. (Teacher one)

> I usually include discussions about environmental topics in my teaching. They seem to interest students quite a lot ... we can go on forever ... I'm surprised how informed students are about these issues. (Teacher two)

References to academic subjects during club activities is purely incidental although the skills learned, particularly communication skills, have had a positive effect on the pupils' academic abilities. Nevertheless, when asked whether she considered the Green Club's activities as curricular or extra-curricular, the headteacher opted for the former without hesitation:

> I don't view what the club does as being extra ... but an integral part of a girl's education. My office overlooks one of the sites in which the club works ... I really admire one particular girl who comes in very early and starts working there ... it is obvious that whatever she's doing stems from an internal value.

The coordinating teacher commented on this internalisation of values when she referred to the 'pleasant surprise' of seeing how the values promoted by the club are observed by pupils who are not club members:

> To be honest, I did not expect the extent to which the objectives that I wanted to achieve through the club have been attained. There's been a ripple effect extending beyond the club's members and over to other students and also to teachers.

The resources used in the project are mainly human resources: two teachers, one of whom is the coordinating teacher ultimately responsible for the club, several other supporting teachers and pupil club members.

Culture and ethos: social and organisational aspects

Ensuring a high quality education is the main target of all Maltese junior lyceums, and especially for this school, which has a very long academic tradition going back to the turn of the twentieth century. Currently the Maltese educational system is in a state of flux, moving gradually from a traditional monolithic centralised system to a more flexible decentralised one. Consequently most schools lie somewhere along the mechanistic-organic continuum (Table 5.4). St Theresa's is no exception and is based on organisational qualities such as purpose, communication, membership and leadership it tends towards the organic. The headteacher's leadership style is a major influence on the organic element of this classification. Although she frequently has to complete the traditional chores associated with a managerial leadership style (Table 5.5) imposed by the central educational authority, she is keen to switch to a democratic style, which is more in harmony with her personal values.

The school is open to any initiative which contributes towards the attainment of a high quality education. This is why, as the headteacher pointed out, the activities carried out during breaktime are varied and numerous. Nevertheless, the values that the Green Club has tried to foster are gradually establishing themselves within the school's culture and ethos. This has been achieved by directly and indirectly involving the club's activities. Although the club is made up of twenty pupil volunteers, less than two per cent of the school population, its activities target all pupils, school staff and parents and it has become part of normal school life.

> The Green Club is not just a club ... it's more of a strategy for environmental awareness that targets the whole school ... the break is mostly used for debriefing. (Coordinating teacher)

> You can easily see the difference that the club has made in the school. The school is cleaner and plants make it more beautiful. (Headteacher)

The most immediate and evident impact of the club has been the embellishment of the school grounds. The waste management strategy adopted by the school has been in effect for some time and waste separation and recycling have become practices accepted by the whole school community. The cleaners have cooperated by changing their work patterns to align these with environmentally sensitive waste management practices. Encouraging pupils to plant and care for potted plants in their classrooms and in the school corridors has enhanced the aesthetics of the school. Parents comment positively on these aesthetics, considering them to be a feature of the school's overall image:

> One thing that immediately strikes you as soon as you enter the school is its sense of cleanliness ... I've got another child who attends another school and the difference is striking. (Parent one)

> Plants, cleanliness and order everywhere ... that is why when something is not in its place it stands out. Even the colour scheme used is an eye opener ... I feel that this sense of good feeling is important considering that our children spend almost a whole day in these corridors. (Parent two)

The club developed the nature patch by reclaiming an abandoned area of ground and converting it into a garden for indigenous plants. The garden serves the dual function of providing a place where students can relax as well as perform fieldwork activities related to their studies. Even pupils who are not Green Club members have internalised certain environmental values which they are keen to defend:

> I organised a debate during which I made students believe that we had received a request to convert the abandoned soil patch into a car park from which the school could also get some revenue. Students were against the idea of just having economic considerations determining the future of their school environment. They pointed out social as well as environmental considerations that should be considered in the decision-making ... mind you these were not club member! (Coordinating teacher)

The Maltese education authorities expect all state schools to prepare an annual School Development Plan (SDP) that highlights targets for schools in their efforts to ensure a good quality of school life. The remit of the SDP ranges from curricular matters to organisational and logistic issues. The headteacher was quick to point out that:

> Environmental matters feature in the SDP... and although these concerns are shared by all the school, they are the Green Club's main concern.

Another requirement of the Maltese education authorities is the Performance Management Programme (PMP) that every teacher has to prepare for him/herself. The PMP outlines a teacher's main targets for his/her professional development. Although both the SDP and the PMP were imposed on the educational community, their impact has been positive in that they have compelled schools and teachers to reflect on and actively plan for their development, rather than leaving this to chance.

During the implementation phase of St Theresa's SDP the coordinating teacher was asked by the headteacher to address her colleagues during a staff development seminar about the need to address environmental concerns in the SDP. Instead of opting for a traditional presentation consisting of a series of arguments to defend territory and drive a message home, she structured her presentation around the results of a questionnaire survey. She had conducted this survey with the whole school community: pupils, teachers, administrative and management staff and cleaners.

> The questionnaire results clearly showed that children and cleaners (who regularly support the club's initiatives) were more aware of the need to act on environmental issues ... This might have been instrumental in helping teachers reflect on their practice and to focus on green matters in their PMP ... It certainly drove me to start targeting teachers more during assembly. (Coordinating teacher)

Pupils were also interviewed about their school's environmental stance. Responses showed that although environmental values are gradually being integrated into the school's ethos, the need for pupils to take an active, participative role in these issues as well as the development of the whole school is still not sufficiently recognised. However Green Club pupil members achieve high levels of participation comparable to levels two and/or three of Hart's ladder of participation (Table 2.1). Although non-club members assume a lower level of participation (level four or five, Table 2.1), they are still reacting to environmental needs rather than being proactive in their actions. In other words, the student population is more willing to follow and cooperate with the club's initiatives, than to take initiatives for themselves. Some peer pressure accounts for this lack of initiative:

> Recycling waste is no big deal. It's very easy because the Green Club makes collection easy. At times I also bring waste paper from home because our locality still lacks bring-in sites for waste. (non Green Club member one)

> On the whole we find a lot of cooperation from our friends. At times we find it very difficult to cope with all the waste paper that they gather! ... You always find a few individuals who are simply not interested or do things on purpose, but on the whole the interest in the environment is present. (Green Club member one)

> No I'm not joining the Green Club ... No it's not that I do not care for the environment, it's just that ... I've heard other students calling them 'nerds' ... and I wouldn't like that to happen to me. (non Green Club member one)

The Green Club wants to promote values which conform with the school's mission of providing students with a holistic education: this is one reason why the initiative to form the club was accepted by senior management. Gradually other teachers who came to share the same environmental values joined the club's ranks. Eventually many people in the school viewed the club's activities as an opportunity to improve the school grounds.

Institutional practice: technical and economic aspects

No resources are specifically allocated to support the club's activities. However, the headteacher does not think twice when it comes to finding financial support for the Green Club's initiatives from the school fund because:

> I feel that I need to support them. I see it as an investment in the overall well-being of the school. Since the club started working I can openly say that the school image has improved.

The human resources required to run the Green Club are huge and apparently lacking. A single teacher who is still ultimately responsible for the club coordinates all the club's functions, no matter how much her club duties are delegated to another teacher helper and club members. Since EE is still not mandatory in the Maltese educational system, space for EE in normal school life is still absent. The lack of time to coordinate, manage and diversify the club's activities is the coordinating teacher's major problem and she would be more than willing to 'trade money for time!' Effective strategies for coping with this time problem have been: initiating routines such as the daily collection of waste for composting, limiting the number of new initiatives and keeping club membership at a manageable level. But the coordinating teacher still has a proactive personal philosophy about resources:

> If I had to wait for money to run the club, then I would still be waiting for it! Although whenever it's available it's more than welcomed, what I value more is the support that I'm given. I have to manage the club over and above my teaching load and approaching someone for help and being told 'Yes' is enough for me ... I've never asked the head for money to cover costs and was turned down ... the school cleaners and handyman are always at my disposal whenever I come up with a crazy idea ... my fellow colleagues (in most of the cases) support the cause.

The coordinating teacher pointed out that parental support for the club was evident, which was encouraging. She is also an active member of a local NGO and musters expertise and teaching resources from this source. The club enjoys a democratic structure and the ideas of every member are given due attention. This allows the club to cater for a variety of pupil needs and learning styles. The underlying emphasis is on the development of a pro-environmental ethic that manifests itself through sustainable actions. The approach the club adopts tends to be problem-oriented. The club decides which issues are worth exploring and considers appropriate ways of acting. Club members are actively invited to discover the dimensions of an environmental issue by gathering information from different sources: the main emphasis is environmental, on the protection of the island's threatened natural heritage, and citizenship and sustainability issues are addressed within this perspective.

The Green Club's objectives are slowly but surely being integrated into the fabric of the school culture. The club set up and managed a waste recycling bank, a compost heap and craft sessions utilising waste: St Theresa's was the first school on the island to adopt recycling practices. The club also organises a yearly *Green Your Classroom Award* for classes that adopt sustainable practices. However, this process has been a constant uphill struggle, despite all the in-school support offered. This integration is still in its infancy and lacks a critical mass of individuals ready to take the initiative and participate actively in developing an environmental ethic for the school. Most of the work still centres on the coordinating teacher. Although she has no intention of stopping, the initiative would most probably lose impetus if she decided to focus on other concerns or to leave the school.

> Unfortunately there's only one (teacher's name). Students look up to her and are very demanding. I'm really concerned that she carries most of the club's weight by herself ... that is why I feel obliged to help the club's activities. (Headteacher)

Self-evaluation

The club has no time for formal evaluation exercises, although there is some informal evaluation and feedback. The club members usually provide the coordinating teacher with feedback gathered from their peers about the impact of specific activities. From this information lessons are learned for the future. The coordinating teacher said that she regularly reflects on the effectiveness of her strategies. In her own words:

> When thinking about how I will organise an activity I always have specific reasons for doing one thing instead of another.

Her way of assessing the success of an initiative is whether her objectives were achieved and at times she was surprised when the impact of an initiative far exceeded her expectations. She knew that:

> I tend to be hard on myself ... I tend to focus more on what else needs to be done rather than what was achieved ... I admit, that looking back quite a lot has been achieved since we started ... but there is still much more to do!

Community links

Maltese schools, especially state schools, have tended to isolate themselves from their surrounding communities, particularly during the 1980s. Any interventions coming from outside were interpreted by schools as an affront to the professionalism of teachers. Regrettably, clashes between schools and their surrounding communities on matters concerning school and curriculum management showed that these suspicions were not always unfounded. This isolation was mostly felt in secondary schools whose pupils came from different parts of the island, so many did not have a sense of belonging to their school's local community.

However, tensions between schools and their communities have thawed somewhat and schools are opening up and sometimes actively forming partnerships with their local communities. For example, although the expenses incurred during the running of the Green Club's activities are met from school funds, BirdLife Malta, a local NGO, has been a resource bank of ideas and inspiration. The current NMC actively encourages the building and consolidation of such community links.

St Theresa's has always been open to the outside, particularly to parents. However, these types of relationship between schools and communities still tend to be examples of the community as guest rather than communities as stakeholders who are jointly responsible with schools for education provision across their communities (see Table 5.6). The Green Club has also contributed to the establishment of links with the community, primarily through the work done with pupils on fostering active and responsible citizenship, but also through the club's indirect impact on parents. Members take an active part in environmental communication outside school through mimes and plays and also by sitting on discussion panels for television/radio programmes.

However since the school's catchment area spans a wide area of the island, there is limited interaction with the community in which the school is located. Nevertheless, the club occasionally organises activities aimed at the community in general. The coordinating teacher admits that a lot more could be done with and for the community, but establishing contacts and coordinating such activities requires a lot of time, of which 'there is always not enough.'

Conclusion

Local research (Pace, 1997b; 2000) has shown that the educational community in Malta considers that EE will only be promoted in the formal education sector if it becomes mandatory in the NMC. An unequivocal EE policy would induce schools such as St Theresa's to integrate and consolidate their efforts in EE and facilitate the assimilation of EE principles into their school ethos, which is what happened when inclusion became a national priority in schools. The publication of the most recent NMC failed to address this need.

The inherent problem is that local policy makers seem confused about what EE is all about. While being familiar with the objectives of EE, they are still unclear about how to achieve them, and simply equate EE with the acquisition of knowledge about the environment (Pace, 1992; Tanti, 2000). Because there is no clear position about what EE entails policy makers continue to harbour misconceptions about it. The most predominant of these misconceptions are that:

- EE is concerned with issues about conserving nature and does not require any social and economic perspectives
- EE is about keeping your surroundings clean – reminiscent of the Maltese government's 1960's *Keep Malta Tidy* campaign
- EE is all about acquiring knowledge and attitudes and has little or nothing to do with putting these into action

To compound the situation, the term EE has been re-proposed in various other forms in Malta for example, biodiversity education, conservation education, ecological education, environment and development education, education for sustainability, and education for sustainable development. This adds to the confusion among educational policy makers who are unfamiliar with the subtleties involved in the academic debates surrounding the use of these terms. This debate also shifts the EE discourse onto a theoretical level that is often far removed from the needs and interests of schools and teachers and relegates EE to the fringes, rather than being at the core of the school community's concerns (Leal Filho and Pace, 2002).

The success of the Green Club is mainly due to the fact that change was initiated from within through a reformatory mode of change (Table 5.7). The initiatives and activities proposed and implemented reflected the needs and concerns of the school community. Rather than waiting for a change in official policy, the Green Club, believing in EE, felt the need for change, desired the change and actively participated in implementing it. Changes in the lifestyles of the school community were gradually introduced over a period of time to allow for acclimatisation and enculturation into new lifestyles. Change was achieved by evolution rather than by revolution (see Chapter Four).

As this case study shows, Maltese schools are gradually shifting their approach to EE to one that respects their *modus operandi*. Rather than opting for the traditional sporadic approach characterised by isolated initiatives organised on a local or a national level, schools are seeking ways of integrating EE into their everyday concerns and activities. This strategy helps to eliminate any mismatch between what is taught as being important and what is important enough to be done (See Chapter Two). This approach irons out double standards and makes the school a more authentic teaching and learning environment.

The shift towards a whole school approach was initially proposed and promoted in schools by environmental NGOs in Malta in the mid 1990s (Grima, 1996; Gatt and Harmsworth, 1998) and is now spreading rapidly to most Maltese schools, particularly through their participation in the Eco-Schools initiative which was launched in the academic year 2002-2003. More and more schools are addressing EE issues in their SDPs and requesting support from the community to implement Local Agenda 21 initiatives (see Chapter Eleven). This grassroots movement will hopefully ensure that the next government curriculum review will include a clear EE policy.

10

Working together, growing together through international collaboration

Fátima Matos Almeida with Tony Shallcross

Introduction

This chapter outlines work in a Portuguese school involved in an international partnership with schools from Belgium, Japan, Russia, Spain and the USA. This partnership receives no financial support, apart from a small amount of money for postage. The project was developed mainly through Internet communication. Since this *Working Together* partnership began in 2001, several scientific themes have developed in the project, all of which have promoted the development and use of school grounds for educational purposes. The project in this Portuguese school had a strong agricultural focus and was supported by the Portuguese Association for Environmental Education (ASPEA), an NGO. The important elements in this project were the enthusiastic teacher and a positive consequence of using English as the international language because it encouraged the communication that promotes the skills pupils need if they are to become planetary citizens. The project started as an extra-curricular initiative, which subsequently had a profound impact on classroom learning and teaching and on the development of a School Agenda 21 plan for the area.

Abstract

1. Description of the School: EB1 Vilarinho School, Cacia, Portugal caters for 26 pupils up to ten years-old in two mixed level classes. One class consists of level one and two pupils, the other of level three and four pupils. The school has three teachers.

2. Aims and Outcomes of the Project

The project relates to the broad aims of environmental education (EE), as referred to in the 1978 UNESCO conference on EE held in Tbilisi and of Portuguese education in general as stated in the Fundamental Act of Education (Ministry of Education, 1986) by promoting:

- caring, adequate and sustainable actions towards nature and the local environment

- children's experimentation with citizenship *in situ*

- the integration of the formal curriculum with aspects of daily community life

- a sense of global community developed through the international partnership

Other project aims were to:

- promote love and care for nature and for farmwork, a very important issue in a rural area such as Vilarinho

- introduce strategies for teaching basic science through experimentation and nature education

3. The Project: Content and Development

Working Together is an international partnership that focuses on group work. It started in Japan in 2001. Water and germination was the first theme to be addressed. Teaching sessions promoted pupils active participation in the process of their own learning. They were asked to complete a set of simple science experiments on a scientific theme such as water and germination. When they had completed these experiments they had to report their findings to pupils in the other countries involved in the *Growing Together* project. Most subjects, such as: Portuguese Language, History, Geography, Maths, Biology and Technology were integrated within the project.

4. Drivers: a) External b) Internal

a) The *Growing Together* project was a clear external, international driver. There was at least one external, national driver. In 2002 the school participated in Portuguese School Agenda 21, which involved schools, education departments, local authorities, health and social care centres in projects concerned with sustainable development.

b) The small class sizes at Vilarinho and the positive attitude of teachers and the school community provided a fertile environment in which the *Growing Together* project flourished. The employment of a specialist project teacher in the school was a particularly strong internal driver.

5. Assessment

The cognitive gain of pupils was reported on by the two class teachers but not assessed in the extra-curricular activities organised by the project teacher.

6. Evaluation
The attitudinal changes of pupils were evaluated, particularly changes in their participation and motivation. Questionnaires were used to collect data and some teaching sessions were videotaped for later viewing and debate. This was formative rather than summative evaluation that did not involve pupils, although pupils were involved in other facets of evaluation.

7. Constraints or Difficulties in Developing the Project
Not every school in Portugal could be involved in the *Working Together* project because of the technology and expertise involved.

8. Benefits of the Project
The development of a positive school ethos and the motivation to continue with the project were the main benefits of *Growing Together*. The project motivated children to learn English and also developed their global understanding and information and communications technology (ICT) skills and competence. The sustainable values and skills that pupils have acquired will become a lifelong resource.

9. Future Developments
The project will continue until the project teacher retires. After that no one knows what will happen.

Research

The action research model used in the project at Vilarinho proved to be a very effective way of evaluating the *Working Together* project. Teachers, pupils and other community groups participated in planning, implementing and evaluating educational activities that aimed to tackle an issue, which all agreed was important. The evaluations demonstrated that the project's outcomes generally corresponded to those agreed by the partners and specified in the project design. For example, there was a general increase in people's awareness of their responsibility for environmental issues. This increased awareness was visible in the participation of the community at large and the school community in particular in the establishment and support of EE projects aimed at the solution to concrete social and environmental problems. By consciously engaging with action, the *Growing Together* project avoided the danger of socialising hypocrisy (see Chapter Two) which can occur when pupil and community awareness is raised without the parallel development of the competences to convert this knowledge into action (Uzzell *et al*, 1994). Pupils played an active part, not only in learning processes but also as active respondents in this action research process (Fielding, 2001).

Class discussions were held towards the end of every school week. In these sessions pupils were encouraged to explain their scientific findings and ideas but also had the opportunity to evaluate the week's individual work and group work, as well as the quality and quantity of the international exchanges that had occurred. The pupils' attitudes towards sharing and their awareness of and willingness to change their local environment were also assessed in these whole school project sessions. The pupils carried out environmental audits of the school and its local community. One indication of the positive impact of the *Working Together* project on children and young people is that many ex-pupils who had worked on the project at Vilarinho, still visit the school to find out about the project's developments and to visit their friends in schools in the other countries involved in the project.

Findings

The project teacher had participated in other environmental projects before coming to teach at Vilarinho School. The isolation of the school and the poverty of the community deprived pupils of significant external stimuli. The two other teachers did not use the Internet, which had only recently been installed in the school, because they did not know how to use it. There were no containers for the separation of waste in the school. This rather bleak situation encouraged the project teacher to organise a project that would improve the school and the social and educational outcomes of its pupils. The project teacher sees herself as an activist who takes an integrated view of change (see Table 5.3) because her teaching is directly concerned with environmental change within the school, its grounds and the local community.

Setting

Vilarinho is a village in the county of Cacia, in the Municipality of Aveiro, in central Portugal. It is on the left bank of the River Vouga, about ten kilometres from the city of Aveiro. The facilities in Vilarinho are limited; there is one cafe, a butcher's shop, two small general shops and a mini-market but no health centre or post office. The people of Vilarinho go to Aveiro or Cacia, another nearby town, to purchase supplies other than food. There is public transport but this operates on a restricted timetable so many people use private transport. Bicycles are still popular for short distances.

Although Vilarinho is close to Aveiro it is still predominantly a rural area whose inhabitants rely on farming. The farmers use some technology, such as tractors, in their daily agricultural work. However, Vilarinho is close to an industrial complex in which companies such as Renault, Funfrap, Vulcano and Portucel employ some of the village's inhabitants. One result of this industrialisation is that Vilarinho is an area at environmental risk. It has high levels of water pollution and despite the presence of a wastewater treatment plant, the River Vouga is still highly polluted.

The Growing Together project

In a rural area, like Vilarinho, where many inhabitants seek employment in local manufacturing industries or emigrate to the nearby towns, it is not surprising that children no longer see farming as an attractive career. Most children consider agricultural tasks to be of minor importance and sometimes despise them as chores. Restoring children's love for the land was a very important aim of the project for the school and the community of Vilarinho. The project aimed to improve pupils' care and respect for farming and nature by encouraging them to do agricultural work themselves and to use the Internet to observe children in the other countries performing similar tasks. In a small way this endeavour sought to develop the pupils as planetary citizens.

The EB1 Vilarinho School is one of a number of schools located in the county of Cacia. The school takes pupils from nursery until they reach lower secondary school age and is housed in two buildings that were built at different times. In the older block there is a classroom for level one and two pupils and an administration room. In the more recent building there are two rooms, one of which is used as a classroom for third and fourth level pupils and the other is used as a multi-purpose room. There are two covered playgrounds and a courtyard with some trees and bushes.

Both classes are mixed, with children of more than one level in the same class: the level one and two class has fifteen pupils and the level three and four class has eleven. Each class has its own teacher and there is also a teacher in charge of project work for all the pupils in the school. Because of the enthusiasm and personal contacts of this project work teacher, the school has been involved in several EE projects that have developed and enhanced its whole school approach to learning and teaching.

Although the *Working Together* project planned to work through the formal curriculum (see Figure 2.1) to reinforce pupils' learning activities, especially in the field of science education at Vilarinho, the project's main activities were scheduled to take place outside regular lessons. To plan for and work on the *Working Together* activities, the project teacher merged the two mixed level classes, creating a group with an age span of four years or more. However, as all three teachers coordinated the different project activities with work inside and outside formal classroom lessons, it soon became clear that the project was not merely an extra-curricular venture as it was affecting classroom learning.

Growing Together clearly demonstrates features of a whole school approach because it responds to the personal, social and educational needs of the pupils as well as the need to reform institutional practices in the school. The school community has developed a policy on sustainability which has been accepted by the school's committee, as a way of putting this whole school philosophy into action. This policy makes recommendations about the content of teaching in the formal curriculum and institutional practices such as the use of water, energy and paper as well as advocating the integration of the formal curriculum with institutional practice (see Figure 2.1).

The international dimension of the *Growing Together* partnership attracted Vilarinho School because it allowed pupils to share learning not only within their own school but also with schools from other countries and even continents. Pupils from different countries discussed their findings, mainly using e-mail. Besides exchanging information about their project activities, children also discussed cultural practices in their countries and learned a lot about each other both as people and citizens as well as pupils. Photographs, essays, seeds and even recipes were exchanged, which allowed pupils from Vilarinho to taste vegetables cooked in the way Japanese children would eat them. Among the Japanese schools that participated in the project were The Earth Club and Ikeda Elementary School. Other schools that participated in the *Working Together* project were the Basic School de Kriebel in Olen, Belgium, the IES (Institute of Secondary Education), A Pinguela from Galicia, Spain, the Northeast Middle School Bethlehem, USA, the Nº23 Dimitrovgrad School, Russia, and the Ulyanovsk School, Russia.

The *Working Together* project was developed through a sequence of themes related to seeds and germination. During the water and germination theme pupils investigated how the everyday use of detergents and soap pollutes ground and surface water on the Earth. Through this theme pupils discovered how pollution inhibits plant growth. The viola theme helped pupils to beautify the school grounds by growing colourful violets, which rapidly became the pride of the whole school. By participating in the *Sakurajima radish contest*, organised by the Office of Sakurajima Island, Japan, pupils were able to compare how the size of this Japanese edible plant varied when it was grown in different soil, water and climatic conditions in the different participating schools around the world. The melon and *go-ya* themes provided the school community with the opportunities to cook and taste both these vegetables. *Go-ya* comes from the island of Okinawa, in the south of Japan, where it is considered to promote health and longevity by the inhabitants of the island, many of whom live to be a hundred years old. Pupils used the Internet to share their experiences of growing several different plants. When sharing this information pupils drew on knowledge from all the curricular areas. Teachers from the Japanese schools coordinated all the themes.

English was the main language used for communication between the partnership schools, although some reports were written in the pupils' own national language and displayed on the Internet. Portuguese primary schools are gradually introducing the teaching of a foreign language, but it is not yet widespread. Vilarinho's experience of linking English teaching with an EE project may prove to be a useful and interesting model. It will be fascinating to see whether learning English at EB1 Vilarinho is enhanced because pupils are using English to communicate about real situations and shared events (Uzzell, 1999) and to communicate with each other about their own developing self-efficacy (Bandura, 1986). The teachers involved used English as the common language in exchanges of e-mails with their international partners. It would be interesting to know whether this process has improved their proficiency in English.

The activities incorporated into *Growing Together* also gave pupils the opportunity to improve their group work because this required active co-operation and participation, regardless of pupils' preferred individual learning styles. The simple activity of planting seeds received from Japanese schools was a memorable experience for the Vilarinho pupils. They had to conduct experiments into the growing conditions required by different plants, the different types of soil and degree of watering required by the particular kinds of seeds they were planting.

Pupils recorded the results of their scientific observations on plant growth at regular intervals. Children with complementary subject or organisational skills were encouraged to work together to help their peers and share knowledge. A small library was installed in a corner of one classroom using books donated by parents, the municipality, NGOs and bookshops. Pupils used these books as well as websites to research themes they were investigating in the *Working Together* project. The pupils recorded their findings on posters and drawings and decorated the walls of their classrooms with them. Drawings took the place of written text when communicating in English proved difficult. At the same time the school's grounds were developed and became more beautiful. Several plots of land were prepared for planting and these were soon filled with the big green leaves of the Sakurajima radish, colourful violets and round white melons.

The schools used the Internet to share their experiences about growing several types of vegetables in their school grounds during the project's water and germination theme. These exchanges produced knowledge and raised issues across all subject areas even though the project's main subject areas were nature education, citizenship and ICT. Many of the flower and vegetable seeds came from Japan: this made the Internet links between the schools more tangible for children. The seeds were the project's control variable, as the children could discuss how identical seeds had fared in different environments.

The pupils from Vilarinho made a presentation about their project and discussed it with their peers from other schools in the municipality on Earth Day 2004 at the first Children's Forum organised by the Portuguese Association for Environmental Education, (ASPEA) in Aveiro. They prepared posters and drawings to show at the forum and were happy to discuss their findings. Photographs and written comments on this event enhanced the school's website.

Through their involvement in the water and germination theme pupils identified the link between the real issue of water contamination in Vilarinho and its effect on the growth of plants. In the school year 2003/04 the water and germination theme was followed by a theme on solid waste that complemented much of the work already done on the first theme. The Spanish partner from Galicia, a member of the Iberoamerican and Caribbean network of Environmental Education (RIACA), a section of Caretakers of the Environment that focuses on making links between Latin-American countries and Spain and Portugal, organised a joint art and design project that complemented the subject focus of *Growing Together*.

This art and design project named *Arte de Sobra* (Art from Waste) was part of the general RIACA program *Puentes* (Bridges). Art from Waste encouraged all the participating schools to use waste to produce artwork and to photograph this artwork and edit the images before they were exchanged over the Internet. Incorporating art and design into the solid waste theme not only changed attitudes towards waste disposal in Vilarinho School but also actions. Because of the Art from Waste project the school started to separate waste and sort it into appropriate containers. The experience of the project added a new aesthetic and creative dimension to EE teaching in all the schools participating in the *Working Together* project.

Another strand of whole school development was Vilarinho School establishing links with its community (Figure 2.1), by inviting members of the local community to become part of the project. This is an example of the community becoming a guest in the school (see Table 5.6). Parents and other relatives of children in the school were invited to participate and the school also collaborated with a range of local institutions and other schools in the county of Cacia to develop a School Agenda 21 plan (see Chapter Eleven) for the Municipality of Aveiro (Quarrie, 1992, Chapter 36). The aim of this plan is to encourage the Municipality's schools to integrate the ecological, economic and socio-cultural issues of Agenda 21 and make them a component of interdisciplinary teaching, while promoting a whole school approach to EE. This plan, which has been partly developed from the internal experiences of schools, is intended to become an external driver for the development of whole school approaches to EE in schools in the Municipality of Aveiro.

Municipalities in Portugal are encouraged to write their own Local Agenda 21 plan and to help schools to write an action plan to address different environmental and development objectives such as:

■ active information in environmental matters

■ environmental information and action at all levels of education

■ cooperation between educational establishments, enterprises and local authorities to solve identified problems

■ increased environmental consciousness in the school community

Vilarinho School's involvement with School Agenda 21 started the school's development as an agent of change in its local community (see Table 5.6). ASPEA in Aveiro coordinated the development of this plan. The first step towards School Agenda 21 was to gather a large group of representatives from schools, youth institutions, parents' unions, universities, the regional departments of the Ministry of the Environment and Ministry of Education and local authorities. The purpose was to establish a joint protocol that would promote regular meetings and a commitment to write a School Agenda 21 plan for all the schools in the area of Aveiro. This is a huge task that will require time.

Conclusion

Since it started in 2001, the main focus of *Growing Together* has been on planting and growing plants, particularly Japanese varieties, and on using ICT for international networking. Gardening in Vilarinho has become less of a chore for children, as it now provides a common base for international scientific experiments and recording and analysing data. The seed varieties change each year. Teachers and pupils always have a voice in the development of the project and take every opportunity to publicise the project to the public, by participating in forums or conferences or giving interviews on local radio programmes. The project was not difficult to develop, as the partners enrolled voluntarily and all the partners accepted the coordination of the project by Japanese teachers.

The project teacher at Vilarinho provided the focus for *Growing Together* in the school; this is the project's strength. But project teachers are rare in Portuguese schools. Most support teachers are used to help improve individual pupils' skills in Language and Maths while working in lessons taught by specialist teachers. However, having a project teacher at Vilarinho is also a weakness because it is not clear what will happen to the *Growing Together* project when this teacher retires. Another problem for Portuguese schools wishing to participate in ICT-focused projects is that no money is allocated to primary schools for computer maintenance, although all schools have computers with Internet links. Sometimes when computers need to be repaired there is no money to pay for repairs. Often there is no teacher in a primary school with the appropriate ICT skills to use computer technologies in the curriculum or anyone who can solve the technical problems that arise with computers.

So planting seeds and watching them grow may serve a bigger purpose than a simple story of the educational impacts of the *Growing Together* project can show. Does this relatively simple project show that one key to restoring the links with the natural world might be by growing plants to meet our needs not only for food, but for beauty and companionship? The beanstalk effect may lie in the power of projects such as *Growing Together* to develop more globally aware and tolerant planetary citizens: effects that are not easily measured by test scores and attainment.

11

Where now and with what help and support?

Tony Shallcross and Fátima Matos Almeida

Introduction

Chapter Four stressed the need for school-focused professional development to support whole school approaches to EE/ESD. However, the vast majority of schools will not have the time, resources or expertise to develop such programmes without outside assistance from local or national education authorities or NGOs. The supportive role that a school inspector can play in helping a school to initiate a whole school approach was very clear in the Greek case study described in Chapter Eight. The Finnish case study described in Chapter Seven is probably the best example in this book of policy support from national government for whole school approaches to EE[13].

There are courses run by many universities in Europe up to masters and doctoral level in EE/ESD. There are also courses organised by the European Commission (EC), the Council of Europe and national and local governments or education authorities and training programmes run by local, national and international NGOs such as the World Wide Find for Nature (WWF). Chapter Ten illustrates how the Portuguese Association of Environmental Education (ASPEA) became involved in training programmes that helped to develop a whole school approach. Unfortunately there is no space to describe the multitude of national, regional, provincial or local initiatives in EE/ESD and/or whole school development that exist across the many and varied countries of Europe. This chapter outlines international initiatives that operate at a global level as well as initiatives that originate from or are

177

based in Europe. These initiatives address five broad areas of relevance to EE/ESD: policy, projects, resources, networks and courses. Even at this international scale it is impossible to identify every project, so only a sample of initiatives can be mentioned in this chapter. Only programmes and initiatives that support or promote EE/ESD and whole school development are examined in detail.

Planetary level provision
Agenda 21

The United Nations Conference on Environment and Development at Rio de Janeiro in 1992 was attended by most of the world's political leaders. It focused attention on the critical issues of sustainability and natural resources and established a plan of action for future global partnerships to achieve concrete goals. Agenda 21 was one of five documents produced by this 1992 Earth Summit which were:

- the Rio Declaration on Environment and Development
- a statement of principles to guide sustainable management of forests
- United Nations Framework Convention on Climate Change
- The Convention on Biological Diversity
- Agenda 21

Agenda 21 is the global partnership for sustainable development, so called because when it was established it aimed to address the problems of the 20th century whilst 'preparing the world for the challenges of the next century' (Quarrie, 1992: 46). Although Agenda 21 fully acknowledges that individual nations cannot achieve sustainable development on their own, the Earth Summit stated that the successful implementation of Agenda 21 was 'first and foremost the responsibility of Governments' (Quarrie, 1992: 46). All European Union governments signed up to Agenda 21, which obliged them to produce national and local Agenda 21 plans by 1997. The strategy behind Agenda 21 was divided into four major sections:

- social and economic dimensions
- conservation and management of resources for development
- strengthening the role of major groups
- means of implementation

Agenda 21 is the plan that guides business and government policies into the 21st century. Population growth, consumption and technology were identified as the primary driving forces of environmental change. Agenda 21 proposes what needs to be done to reduce wasteful and inefficient consumption patterns in some parts of the world whilst carefully managing natural resources. Action programmes for the coming century have to be prepared by each nation and be applied at different levels: hence the term Local Agenda 21. There are roles for everyone: governments, business people, trade unions, scientists, teachers, indigenous people, women, youth and children.

Education was addressed under Section Four in Chapter 36. This chapter was entitled: *Promoting education, public awareness and training*. The first section of Chapter 36 headed *Re-orienting Education Towards Sustainable Development*, states:

> Both formal and non-formal education are indispensable in changing peoples' attitudes so that they have the capacity to assess and address their sustainable development concerns. It is critical for achieving environmental and ethical awareness, values and attitudes, skills and behaviours consistent with sustainable development and for effective public participation in decision-making. (Quarrie, 1992: 221)

Although Chapter 36 makes no specific reference to whole school development it recognises education as a process that will improve the 'capacity of the people to address environment and development issues' (Quarrie, 1992: 221). The recognition that 'both formal and non-formal education are indispensable to changing peoples' attitudes' could be taken as implicit support for approaches to EE/ESD with strong community links and effective participation in decision-making. The 1992 Earth Summit and the preparatory work done on education policy have had a profound effect on the development of EE, such as the growth in the use of the term ESD in preference to EE. As Stokes *et al* (2001), observed when discussing the development of EE in educational systems in the EU:

> Early views focused on changing ecosystems and the impact of various forms of pollution. However, the social, economic and cultural dimensions of the environment have been increasingly recognised and the inclusion of sustainable development makes the concept even more broad. (4)

Two other impacts of the 1992 Earth Summit were:

- the integration of development and environmental issues, leading to the increased use of the term ESD

179

■ the adoption by most world governments of a binding resolution on a range of environmental and development issues, including education and Agenda 21, to deal with these issues

Many environmental and development organisations worked together to write statements and policies for consideration at the 1992 Earth Summit. One of the most influential of these documents was *Caring for the Earth* (1991) produced by IUCN, UNEP and WWF. This document placed great emphasis on education as a key factor in building sustainable societies, such as:

■ Action 3.4. Provide universal primary education for all children and reduce illiteracy (25)

■ Action 6.2. Review the status of environmental education and make it an integral part of formal education at all levels (54)

■ Action 6.3: Determine the training needs for a sustainable society and plan to meet them (55)

The 2002 Earth Summit in Johannesburg reinforced ESD by emphasising the need to integrate sustainable development perspectives at all levels in societies and to promote education as a decisive factor for change. Another significant milestone that influenced EE/ESD was the UN's (2000) Millennium Development Goals (MDG), which set clear targets for global sustainable development in the 21st century. The three MDGs most relevant to EE/ESD are:

■ the achievement of universal primary education
■ ensuring environmental sustainability
■ establishing a global partnership for sustainable development

Whilst not explicitly advocating whole school development in EE/ESD, these global educational developments provide support for the principles of whole school approaches to EE/ESD outlined in this book.

The UN Decade of ESD (2005-2014)

The UN declared 2005-2014 the Decade of ESD (DESD) and there have already been a number of events organised by institutions and organisations across the world to support the aims of this decade. Similarly to the UN's approach to the implementation of the recommendations of the Earth Summits, the responsibility for implementation of the DESD lies with national governments and other national and international civil society organisations such as NGOs. The DESD has five objectives:

- to give an enhanced profile to the central role of education and learning in the common pursuit of sustainable development
- to facilitate links and networking, exchange and interaction among stakeholders in ESD
- to provide a space and opportunity for refining and promoting the vision of, and transition to sustainable development through all forms of learning and public awareness
- to foster increased quality of teaching and learning in ESD
- to develop strategies at every level to strengthen capacity in ESD (UNESCO, 2004)

The Draft International Implementation Scheme (UNESCO, 2004) for the DESD identifies 'three key areas of sustainable development – society, environment and economy with culture as an underlying dimension' (5). The DESD's vision of education is one that integrates formal, non-formal and informal education. The Draft Implementation Strategy argues that the processes of 'learning/teaching in ESD must model the values of sustainable development itself' (21) and that ESD should be reflected in daily decisions and actions. It goes on to state that ESD should be interdisciplinary, holistic, values-driven, critical, multi-method, participatory and locally relevant. This vision of ESD gives clear support for whole school approaches. More information on the UN DESD can be found at http://portal.unesco.org/education/en/

UNESCO have also sponsored a teacher education programme: *Teaching and learning for a sustainable future* that is available on-line at url: http://www.unesco.org/education/tlsf and contains 25 teacher education modules on ESD for use by trainees and practising teachers. The UN DESD is linked to other international educational initiatives or initiatives that involve education, '...in particular the Millennium Development Goals (MDG) process, the Education for All (EFA) movement and the United Nations Literacy Decade (UNLD) (UNESCO, 2004: 12).

EU initiatives in whole school development in EE/ESD
EU policy and practice in EE/ESD

In 1988, the Ministers of Education in Europe issued a joint declaration on EE, which stated that EE should be based on certain common principles:

- the environment is the common heritage of humanity
- humans have a duty to maintain, protect and improve the quality of the environment
- prudent and rational use of natural resources.
- finding ways in which each individual can, particularly by his/her own actions, contribute to the protection of the environment (Council and Ministers of Education, 1988)

While this declaration was not binding on member governments of the EU, it was influential in the development of EE/ESD strategies in many European countries. However, progress was slow and in 1995 a European Union briefing reviewing the development of EE concluded that some national decisions still raised obstacles for EE, such as constraints on space and school time and the lack of recognition that EE could prepare people for future employment. This briefing paper (Commission for the European Communities, Staff Working Paper, 1995) clearly identified the following major difficulties in implementing EE:

- delays in the initial training of teachers
- lack of funding to accompany training courses and the implementation of projects
- the difficulty of organising interdisciplinary work
- the complexity of environmental problems, which are in a state of constant evolution
- lack of expertise in handling the teaching materials and information, which are available in large quantities but are not always suited to requirements

In 2003 the United Nations Economic Commission for Europe organised a meeting of ministers of the environment from Europe, Canada and the USA, which examined the need to improve ESD in educational systems. The ministers identified five key principles in achieving this improvement:

- ESD is a cross-sectoral issue encompassing economic, environmental and social dimensions and demanding a *participatory* and *holistic* approach

- learners at all levels should be encouraged to use *critical thinking* and *reflection* as a prerequisite for concrete action
- sustainable development should be addressed by all educational programmes at all levels; including vocational education and continuing education
- education is a lifelong process involving *formal, non-formal* and *informal* education
- the overall aim of sustainable development is to *empower citizens* to *act for positive* and *environmental change* and this implies a *process-oriented* and *participatory approach* (Ministry of Education and Science, 2004: 10)

(We have italicised sections of the five principles that have been specifically mentioned as features of whole school approaches in this book.)

Most European countries have an official statement on EE/ESD. Some of the five case studies in Chapters Six to Ten refer to these policies. The age, completeness and effectiveness of these policies vary, but where they exist they form an important backdrop to the development of school policies and practices in EE/ESD (see Chapter Nine). Some policies specifically mention whole school approaches (DfES, 2003).

At best these policies are the source of a cascade of statements and policies on curriculum structure and content, teaching and learning practice and school organisation. At worst they are nearly forgotten documents, produced to meet a political need and never given the resources and support required to implement them. They form much of the background to EE/ESD in European countries and often determine which of the two terms, EE/ESD, is used in each country. The policies have been developed to different extents by governments and educational administrators and sometimes provide a statutory framework for school provision in EE/ESD.

The EU has provided policy support for EE/ESD by initiatives such as the Conference on Environmental Security (2004), the Second Conference on Education and Health Partnerships (2001) and a report on EE in the educational systems of EU countries (Stokes *et al*, 2001). All are available through the Europa website: http://europa.eu.int/index_en.htm

Through the European Commission (EC) the EU provides financial support for school partnerships, networks, curriculum development projects, teacher and student exchanges and joint course developments in EE/ESD. The organisation responsible for funding these initiatives is SOCRATES, the

Directorate for Education and Training. There are two strands of funding that are relevant to EE/ESD in schools:

- COMENIUS, which funds projects that focus on school education
- ERASMUS, which focuses on higher education, including some aspects of teacher education

Information about these two funding streams can be found at: www.europa. eu.int/comm/education/socrates

This chapter examines two examples of COMENIUS-funded projects that are specifically relevant to whole school development in the fields of EE/ESD.

COMENIUS Network: School Development through Environmental Education (SEED) (www.seed-eu.net)

The COMENIUS thematic SEED network consists of fourteen European partner countries and six member countries, including some from outside Europe: Australia, Canada, Japan, Korea and New Zealand. SEED's theme is the link between school development and EE/ESD. The purpose of the network is to encourage cooperation among partners by organising meetings, seminars and conferences and producing publications. The aims and objectives of SEED are:

- to promote EE as a driving force for school development
- to facilitate European school systems preparing for the UN DESD 2005 – 2014
- to encourage co-operation among stakeholders in current, completed and prospective COMENIUS projects
- to invite schools, teacher education institutes and education authorities to work together, to learn from each other's experiences and thus to accumulate their knowledge
- to enhance face-to-face communication and virtual communication as bases for a joint progression of ESD in national educational systems (Based on www.seed-eu.net: page on aims and objectives)

There are very close links between SEED and the OECD/ENSI network discussed later in this chapter.

COMENIUS Teacher education project: Sustainability Education in European Primary Schools (SEEPS) (www.education.ed.ac.uk/esf)

SEEPS is a continuing professional development (CPD) project designed to assist trainee and practising teachers to promote whole school approaches to EE/ESD in their schools. This project adopts a school-focused approach to CPD by providing materials to support teachers in the development of whole school approaches in their own schools, after a member of staff has been trained in the use of the project materials (see Chapter Four).

The SEEP's vision of whole school approaches is a process-based vision in which the emphasis is on how pupils are educated while outcomes are deliberated, decided and practised at a local level. The project takes a liberal humanist view of CPD, which means that although alternative theories, principles and models are referred to in the project, it is left to individual schools and teachers to decide on the ideological perspective that should underpin ESD in their own school/classroom context. All the authors who have contributed chapters to this book have either been involved in the development of the SEEPS project materials or have attended COMENIUS in-service training courses in the use of the project materials. The project is available in two forms:

- A CD-Rom that is aimed at schools and practising teachers: *School Development Through Whole School Approaches to Sustainability Education* (Shallcross, 2004). Copies of this CDRom are available to accredited teacher education organisations and institutions from: Dr. Tony Shallcross, Institute of Education, Manchester Metropolitan University, Crewe Green Rd., CREWE CW1 5DU, UK e-mail: a.g.shallcross@mmu.ac.uk

- A website for initial teacher education *Educating for Sustainable Futures* www.education.ed.ac.uk/esf or www.mmu.ac.uk/ioe (showcase)

Achieving balance on the continuum between indoctrination-prescription-suggestion and discovery has been a constant feature of the debate surrounding the development of the SEEPS materials. The activities and materials included in the text are intended to be illustrative exemplars. School staff are encouraged to adapt activities and resources to suit their own context in the spirit of situated professional learning (see Chapter Two). To facilitate this process, text and diagrams can be copied into word files from the CD-Rom or the website, so that materials and/or activities can be modified and/or translated electronically. Fullan's (1991, 1992, 1993, 1995

Table 11.1: SEEPS Project: unit titles and outlines

Unit	Outline
0: Introduction and whole school approaches	This unit introduces the philosophy and school-focused model of professional development used in the project. It has activities designed to introduce some of the key features of whole school approaches and development.
1: Why bother with sustainability education?	This unit has eight possible starting points for a school wishing to develop a whole school approach to ESD. The eight sections encourage school staff to examine the implications of each starting point for a whole school development programme in their own school. Each activity allows reflection on current and/or future practices.
2: Values, attitudes and	Most national policies or strategies on EE/ESD make specific reference to changing values and attitudes as part of the process of achieving sustainable actions. This unit looks at some approaches to values education in schools both inside and outside the classroom. It also examines some techniques for assessing attitudinal change. The focus is not just on the attitudes of pupils but also on those of staff and schools.
3: Culture and sustainability	Culture influences the way we make sense of the environment. It affects our use of the world and its natural resources. Cultural diversity is one of Europe's riches; it is reflected in diet, landscape, art and many other facets of life. The European dimension comes through most strongly in this unit, in which case studies and a variety of cultural examples are used to explore cultural links with the environment in both classroom and whole school approaches. The unit asks whether the achievement of sustainable lifestyles requires cultural change.
4: Leading and managing change	This unit consists of a set of materials to help trainers to anticipate and deal with many of the internal issues that arise in the process of educational change, such as surveying current practice, preparing action plans and analysing change. This unit is at the heart of the project. Different models of change are described so that change can be examined from multiple perspectives.
5: Teaching through the environment	This unit focuses on classroom practice. It advocates cross-curricular approaches and looks at how the environment can be used as a stimulus for teaching and how whole school development can start with the formal curriculum. It adopts an ideology of children based on the concepts of multiple intelligence and active citizenship. The unit considers how the

186

	environment can be used as a starting point for teaching in three areas: science and maths, language and creative subjects and humanities and social sciences. The examples given aim at seven to ten year old pupils but many of these approaches can be adapted for use with older or younger pupils.
6: Self-evaluation, action research and whole school approaches	This unit looks at evaluation and advocates more self-evaluation of whole school approaches. Evaluation is one of five key strands of whole school approaches. The unit looks at a range of approaches to evaluation and advocates the involvement of pupils and the community in evaluating how successful whole school approaches are.
7: Case studies	This unit contains case studies from a number of European countries, mainly drawn from schools trying to develop whole school approaches. The unit also provides guidelines for schools to develop their own case studies. This unit provides much of the contextual knowledge that is at the heart of school-focused CPD.

and 1999) organic rather than mechanistic views of educational change are important signposts for the project and particularly for the unit on managing change. Table 11.1 describes the titles and outlines the content of each unit in the SEEPS Project.

Other European based initiatives
Organisation for Economic Cooperation and Development
Environment and School Initiatives (OECD/ENSI) (www.ensi.org)

The ENSI secretariat is currently based in Switzerland. It is an international government-based network that concentrates on the international exchange of experiences about innovation and research in EE and ESD. ENSI is closely linked to the SEED network and is developing an official partnership with UNESCO to support the work for the UN DESD. The ENSI network adopts a participatory approach to bring schools, education authorities, teacher education institutions and organisations, educational researchers and others interested in EE/ESD together. ENSI has a strong focus on action research and school development that promotes environmental understanding, active approaches to teaching and learning and citizenship education. Its membership is drawn from more than twenty countries worldwide, though currently over 60 per cent of the countries represented in ENSI are from Europe. ENSI's main strengths are that it is:

- institution based, representing national education authorities at senior government level

- a research-oriented network, involving research institutions sharing an active and participative vision of educational research in EE/ESD

- action-oriented, fostering school initiatives and projects that seek to develop the quality of schooling in the community and ensure that this is consistent with the concept of sustainable development

ENSI's main areas of work include: initiating, coordinating and supporting research and school development activities; promoting international exchange, understanding and cooperation, including cooperating with other international organisations and programmes; and making policy recommendations or statements on EE/ESD.

ENSI's major project areas are:

- teacher education

- mainstreaming EE in the school curriculum;

- learnscapes

- Quality Criteria for Ecoschools (Breiting *et al*, 2005) and the SEED network

(This section was based on www.ensi.org. page on definitions.)

Foundation for Environmental Education (FEE) (www.fee-international.org)

FEE, formerly the Foundation for Environmental Education in Europe, is an international NGO aiming to promote sustainable development through EE. It concentrates on formal school education, staff training and raising environmental awareness. FEE has member organisations in 41 countries in Africa, Asia, Australasia, Europe and North and South America that administer one or more of FEE's five main programmes. In order to become a full member of FEE an organisation has to implement at least two of FEE's five main programmes in full. These five programmes are:

- *Eco-Schools*: an environmental management, certification and ESD programme for schools

- *Young Reporters for the Environment*: a secondary school network in which each school investigates an environmental issue and reports relevant information to the public

- *Learning about Forests*: encourages schools to use forests for educational activities

188

- *Blue Flag*: an environmental labelling award for beaches, marinas and boats
- *Green Key*: an eco-labelling system for tourist facilities such as hotels, restaurants and campsites that practise sustainable tourism

(Based on the www.fee-international.org, about us pages.)

It is the first three of these programmes, especially the first, that are of interest in promoting whole school development in EE/ESD. National NGOs have implemented the *Eco-schools* programme in many EU countries and in some countries schools are awarded a green flag for outstanding achievements in environmental management and ESD.

Conclusion

Although whole school development must be sensitive to local contexts, no school is an isolated island (Table 5.6) when it is developing a whole school programme. This chapter has outlined potential sources of international, external sources of support to assist schools in developing whole school approaches to EE/ESD. Chapters Seven and Ten illustrate some of the benefits and problems of being involved in international networks, but networks and support for EE/ESD and whole school development are often are available at local, regional and national levels. As Chapters Three and Five indicate, most successful change involves a top-down element, even though the process of whole school development is based on a grassroots bottom-up strategy. We hope that this book inspires you and your school to set out on this journey towards sustainability.

Notes

1   Performance and Assessment (PANDA) reports provide an overview of each school's performance in relation to other schools using data from Ofsted, the Department for Education and Skills (DfES) and the Qualifications and Curriculum Authority (QCA).

2   The term sustainable development and differences and similarities between the terms EE and ESD are examined in the Introduction.

3-7   Refer to the Introduction for some clarification of these terms

8   Coppice club is an after school club run for children.

9,12   Refer to the Introduction for clarification of these terms

10,13 Refer to the Introduction for clarification of the terms EE and education for sustainable development ESD

11   Paradigm is used in these quotes to mean example

Author biographies

Fátima Matos Almeida: Special education teacher, co-founder of ASPEA – *Portuguese Association for Environmental Education* in 1990. President of ASPEA since 1992 and member of the board of Caretakers of the Environment International. Participated in several EU projects, such as ECONET (School Agenda 21), URBANET (Urban Environment) and SEEPS (Sustainability Education). Co-coordinator of the Art and Environment Programme and co-organiser, since 1993 of the 3-day annual ASPEA conference on EE. Accredited as a teacher trainer by the Portuguese Council of In-service training in the area of Educational and EE Projects and Special Education, participated in many teachers training courses since 1996.

Dr Christopher Bezzina: lecturer at the Faculty of Education, University of Malta. Course leader of the International and Maltese Masters programme in Educational Leadership. Involved with a wide range of schools on school development and school improvement initiatives. Has done consultancy work in the professional development of teachers and educational leaders in Malta, Italy, Latvia, Lithuania, Poland, Sweden, the Seychelles and the United States. Fulbright Scholar in 2004 at the State University of New York at Buffalo where he conducted research into schools as learning communities. Involved in a number of European bodies and a Member of the European Network for Teacher Education Policies (ENTEP), Administrative Council Member of the Association for Teacher Education in Europe (ATEE), Executive Council Member of the Commonwealth Council for Educational Administration and Management (CCEAM). Current President of the Malta Society for Educational Administration and Management (MSEAM) and represents Malta in the European Commission Cluster group on Teachers and Trainers. Appointed visiting professor at the University of Bologna in educational leadership.

Pat McDonnell: Headteacher of Smallwood School with a keen interest in whole school development. She has taught in a wide variety of primary schools and also been a secondary teacher of English. Attended the COMENIUS in-service courses: *Creating a better environment in our school,* in the UK in 1999.

Hanna Niiranen-Niittylä: MA (Education) University of Turku, a primary school teacher and qualified special education teacher (University of Turku, 2005). who has attended two COMENIUS in-service courses: *Creating a better environment in our school*, in the UK and *E-learning and the Internet*, Germany. Coordinated the COMENIUS Project Environmental Education in Europe, 2000-2003. Won The Arts Council of Southwest Finland's special prize for Art Education at School in 2002. A committed an enthusiastic teacher of EE.

Dr. Paul Pace, (B.Ed. (Hons.), M Ed., Ph.D.): Director of CEER (Centre for Environmental Education and Research). Active in EE as chairperson of Malta's National Environmental Education Strategy, founder of the Malta Association of Environmental Educators and as a researcher at the Faculty of Education, University of Malta where he is a senior lecturer in EE and science education. Appointed EkoSkola National Coordinator for Nature Trust (Malta), and a member of the National Commission for Sustainable Development and vice-chair of the Environment Commission of the Maltese Archdiocese. Involved in several local and foreign projects aimed at the development of curriculum material for EE and works actively with teachers in the implementation of environmental and science school policies.

John Robinson (B. Ed. (Hons.), M.A. Econ., M. Ed., M. Phil): Director of Research Development in the Centre for Urban Education at Manchester Metropolitan University, UK. Began teaching in secondary schools in Manchester, Glasgow and Salford. Since joining Crewe and Alsager College of Higher Education and especially since the merger with Manchester Metropolitan University in 1992, has been involved in a range of research focused on a diverse range of issues including evaluation research, teacher education research, post-compulsory education policy, multicultural education and cross-curricular themes, particularly EE and sustainability education. Part of research team which evaluated GridClub, contracted by the British Educational Communications and Technology Agency (Becta). Has published numerous articles and book chapters and is co-editor of *Educational Studies: Critical issues and Perspectives* (Open University Press, 2006 with Derek Kassem and Emmanuel Mufti.

Dr. Tony Shallcross (BA Hons, MEd, PhD): Principal Lecturer, Head of International Education and designated researcher at the Institute of Education Manchester Metropolitan University. Over twenty years experience of teaching in schools involving senior academic and pastoral posts of responsibility. Current responsibilities include teaching on initial teacher education (primary and secondary) and CPD, including course direction for EC funded COMENIUS CPD courses. Research includes funded evaluative research projects for Scottish Natural Heritage, the World Wildlife Fund for Nature, the Institute for Global Ethics, Teacher Training Agency and the National College for School Leadership.

Project director for the EC funded Sustainability Education in European Primary Schools Project (SEEPS). Has published many journal papers and chapters on EE/ESD. Project coordinator of the Department for International Development funded Higher Education link project Promoting Sustainable Development through Whole School Approaches with Rhodes University and the University of South Africa. Former member of UNESCO teacher education group for education for sustainable development.

Konstandia Tamoutseli: earned B.Sc in Horticulture and Ph.D. in Education at Aristotle University of Thessaloniki, Greece, and MPhil in Landscape Architecture at Edinburgh University. For the last nine years, has worked as Advisor for Environmental Education for the Ministry of Education in Thessaloniki, Greece. Lectures at Thrace University in academic areas such as Sustainable Development and Landscape Design and teaches EE at Aristotle University of Thessaloniki. As an advisor of EE, focuses on the empowerment of Greek schools to work out EE projects for the redevelopment of schools. Has published many articles on EE and educational materials and has helped to rejuvenate many schoolyards in Greece according to sustainable standards. Coordinates a national EE network named *My Schoolgrounds,* sponsored by the Greek Ministry of Education.

Dr. Arjen Wals: Associate Professor in the Education and Competence Studies Group of Wageningen University in the Netherlands. Specialises in the areas of EE, participation, communication and interactive policy making. PhD, from the University of Michigan in Ann Arbor, under the guidance of UNESO's first Director for Environmental Education, the late Prof. William B. Stapp, explored the crossroads between EE and environmental psychology. More recent research topics include: the role of conflict in environmental and social change, sustainability in higher education, and the development of critical consumerism. Author and co-author of over 120 publications on EE related issues and serves on the editorial board of four environmental education research journals. Past president of Caretakers of the Environment International.

References

Ainscow, M., Hopkins, D., Southworth, G. and West, M. (1994) *Creating the Conditions for School Improvement*, London: David Fulton

Alderson, P. (2000) Citizenship in Theory and Practice: Being or Becoming Citizens with Rights, in D. Lawton, J. Cairns and R. Gardner (eds) *Education for Citizenship*, London: Continuum

Alexander, R. (1984) *Primary Teaching*, London: Cassell

Argyris, C. and Schön, D.A. (1996) *Organizational Learning II, Theory, Method, and Practice*, Reading, Mass: Addison-Wesley

Aspin, D.N. (1995) The Conception of Democracy: A Philosophy of Democratic Education, in J. Chapman, I. Froumin and D. Aspin (eds) *Creating and Managing the Democratic School*, London and Bristol: The Falmer Press

Ball S.J. (1985) Participant Observation with Pupils in R.G. Burgess (ed) *Strategies of Educational Research: Qualitative Methods*, Falmer Press: Lewes

Ball, S.J. (1987) *The Micro-politics of the School*, London: Methuen

Bandura, A. (1986) *Social Foundations of Thought and Action: A Social Cognitive Theory*, Englewood Cliffs: Prentice Hall

Barth, R.S. (2002) The Culture Builder, *Educational Leadership*, 59(8)

Beane, J.A. and Apple, M.W. (1999) The case for democratic schools, in M.W. Apple and J.A. Beane (eds) *Democratic Schools: Lessons from the chalk face*, Buckingham: Open University Press

Begg, A. (2000) *Empowering the Earth: Strategies for Social Change*, Dartington: Green Books

Benedict, F. (1999) A Systemic Approach to Sustainable Environmental Education, *Cambridge Journal of Education*, 29(3)

Bezzina, C. (1988) *School Development: Heading for Effectiveness in Education*, Malta: MUT Publications

Bezzina, C. (1999) *Opening Doors to School Improvement: an introductory handbook*, Malta: MUT Publications

Bezzina, C. (2002) Rethinking teachers' professional development in Malta: agenda for the twenty-first century, *Journal of In-Service Education*, 28(1)

Bezzina, C. and Pace, P. (2004) Promoting school development through environmental education, in *Trends, Monograph Series in Education*, Issue 1, Malta: University of Malta Faculty of Education

Blenkin, G.M., Edwards G. and Kelly A.V. (1992) *Change and the Curriculum*, London: Phil Chapman Publishing

195

Booth, R. (1987) Thoughts after Moscow, in CEE (Council for Environmental Education), *AREE – Annual Review of Environmental Education*, No.1 – Review of 1987, Reading: CEE

Bouzakis, S. (2000) *Greek Education* (1821-1999), Athens: Gutenberg

Bowers, C.A. (1997) *The Culture of Denial, Why the Environmental Movement Needs a Strategy for Reforming Universities and Public Schools*, Albany: State University of New York Press.

Boyle, D. (2001) Tyranny of Numbers, *Resurgence*, 205

Brain, J. (2001) True Learning, *Resurgence*, 204

Breiting, S. and Mogensen, F. (1999) Action Competence and Environmental Education, *Cambridge Journal of Education*, 29(3)

Breiting, S. Mayer, M. and Mogensen, F. (2005) *Quality Criteria for ESD-Schools: Guidelines to enhance the quality of Education for Sustainable Development*, Vienna: Austrian Federal Ministry of Education

Brighouse, T. (2000) *Birmingham School Leadership Website*, (Online) http://www.bgfl.org/ services/leaders/default.htm

Brighouse, T. and Woods, D. (1999) *How to Improve Your School*, London: Routledge

Burbules, N.C. (2000) Does the Internet Constitute a Global Educational Community? in N.C. Burbules and C.A. Torres (eds) *Globalisation and education: critical perspectives*, New York and London: Routledge

Caldwell, B. and Spinks, J. (1988) *The Self-Managing School*, London: Falmer Press

Capra, F. (1996) *The Web of Life*, New York: Anchor Books

Carr, W. and Kemmis, S. (1986) *Becoming Critical: Education, Knowledge and Action Research*, London: Falmer Press

Carter, A. (1990) On Individualism, Collectivism and Interrelationalism, *Heythrop Journal*, 21

Cassel, P. and Giddens, A. (1993) *The Giddens reader*, Macmillan: Basingstoke

Chaplin, E. (1996) Reengineering in health-care: the four phase work cycle, *Quality Process*, 29 (10)

Clayton, A.M.H. and Radcliffe, N. J. (1996) *Sustainability, A Systems Approach*, London: Earthscan, WWF and The Institute for Policy Analysis

Clover, D. (2002) Traversing the Gap: conscientization, educative activism in environmental adult education, *Environmental Education Research*, 8(3)

Coles, R. (1997) *The Moral Intelligence of Children*, London: Bloomsbury

Commission of the European Communities (1995) *Commission Staff Working Papers: Environmental Education*, Brussels 20/10/95, SEC (95) 1754

Costa, A. and Kallick, B. (2000) Getting into the Habit of Reflection, *Educational Leadership*, 57(7)

Council of Europe (1999) *Everyone can make a difference, Council of Europe Pilot Project on Participation in and through School, Initial Training Seminar for Teachers*, Report, Strasbourg: Council of Europe

Council of Europe (2000) *Everyone can make a difference, Council of Europe Pilot Project on Participation in and through School, Second Training Seminar for Teachers*, Report, Strasbourg: Council of Europe

Council and the Ministers of Education (1988) Resolution of the Council and the Ministers of Education meeting with the Council on Environmental Education of 24 May 1988 88/c 177/03, *Official Journal of the European Communities, Information and Notices*, C177, Vol. 31, 6 July 1988, Luxembourg: Office for Official Publications of the European Communities

Court, M. (2003) *Different Approaches to Sharing School Leadership, International Practitioner Enquiry Report*, Nottingham: National College for School Leadership

Davies, B. (1982) *Life in the Classroom and the Playground: The Accounts of Primary School Children*, Routledge and Kegan Paul: London

Davies, B. and Ellison, L. (1999) *Strategic Direction and Development of the School*, London: Routledge

Davies, L. (1999) Researching democratic understanding in primary school, *Research in Education*, 61

Day, C., Harris, A. and Hadfield, M. (2001) Grounding knowledge of schools in stakeholder realities: a multi-perspective study of effective school leaders, *School Leadership and Management*, 21(1)

Denzin, N.K. (1994) The art and politics of interpretation in N. K. Denzin and Y. S Lincoln (eds) *Handbook of Qualitative Research*, London: Sage

Des Jardins, J.R. (1993) *Environmental Ethics: an introduction to environmental philosophy*, Belmont: Wadsworth

(DfEE) Department for Education and Employment and the (QCA) Qualifications and Curriculum Authority (1999) *Citizenship*, London: QCA

(DfES) Department for Education and Skills (2003) *Sustainable development action plan for education and skills*, London, DfES

Duignan, P. (1998) *Authenticity in Leadership: the rhetoric and the reality, paper presented at the ATEE 23rd Annual Conference*, Mary Immaculate College, Limerick: Ireland, 24-30 August

Du Quesnay, H. (2003) Goodbye compliance, welcome self-reliance, in *The Times Educational Supplement*, London: TLS Education, June 6th

Eden Project (2004) *Little Book of Big Ideas*, London: Eden Project Books

Edwards, A. (1996) Can Action Research Give Coherence to the School Based Learning of Experiences of Students? in C. O' Hanlon (ed) *Professional Development through Action Research in Educational Settings*, London: Falmer Press

Eisner, E.W. (1991) *The Enlightened Eye: Qualitative Inquiry and the Enhancement of Educational Practice*, New York: Macmillan Publishing

Elliott, J. (1991) *Action research for educational change*, Philadelphia: Open University Press

Elliott, J. (1993) What have we learned from action research in school-based evaluation? *Educational Action Research*, 1(1)

Elliot, J. (1999) Sustainable Society and Environmental Education: future perspectives and demands for the education system, *Cambridge Journal of Education*, 29(3)

Elmore, R.F. (2002) Hard questions about practice, *Educational Leadership*, 59(8)

Evans, K. (1993) *School Based Inservice Education: case studies and guidelines for implementation*, Culemborg: Phaedon

Farrer, F. with Hawkes, N. (2000) *A Quiet Revolution: Encouraging positive values in our children*, London: Rider

Fielding, M. (1995) Mapping the progress of change, paper presented at the European Conference on Educational Research, University of Bath, 14-17 September

Fielding, M. (2001) Students as Radical Agents of Change, *Journal of Educational Change* 2(2)

Fielding, M. (2004) Transformative approaches to student voice: theoretical underpinnings, recalcitrant realities, *British Educational Research Journal*, 30(4)

Foster, J. (2001) Education as Sustainability, *Environmental Education Research*, 7(2)

Freeman, C. (1999) Children's participation in environmental decision-making, in S. Buckingham-Hatfield and S. Percy (eds) *Constructing Local Environmental Agendas: People places and participation,* London: Routledge

Fullan, M.G. (1991) *The New Meaning of Educational Change,* London: Cassell

Fullan, M.G. (1992) *Successful School Improvement – The Implementation Perspective and Beyond,* Buckingham: Open University Press

Fullan, M.G. (1993) *Change Forces: Probing the Depths of Educational Reform,* London: Falmer Press

Fullan, M.G. (1995) The limits and potential of professional development, in T.R. Guskey and M. Huberman (eds) *Professional Development in Education: New paradigms and practices,* New York: Teachers College Press

Fullan, M.G. (1999) *Change Forces: the Sequel,* London, Falmer Press

Fullan, M.G. and Hargreaves, A. (1992) *What's Worth Fighting for in Your School?* Buckingham: Open University Press

Gatt, J. and Harmsworth, N. (1998) The Role of Non-Governmental Organisations in Environmental Education in Malta, Unpublished B.Ed. (Hons) dissertation, Malta: Faculty of Education, University of Malta

Germanos, D. (2002) *The Walls of Knowledge: School Environment and Education,* Athens: Gutenberg

Giddens, A. (1979) *Central Problems in Social Theory Action: Structure and Contradiction in Social Analysis,* London: Macmillan

Giroux, H.A. (1996) Towards a Postmodern Pedagogy, in L. Cahoone (ed) *From Modernism to Postmodernism: An Anthology,* Oxford: Blackwell

Glickman, C.D. (2002) *Leadership for Leading: How to help teachers succeed,* Alexandria VA: ASCD

Gold, A., Evans, J., Earley, P., Halpin, D. and Collarbone, P. (2003) Principled principals? Values-driven leadership: evidence from ten case studies of 'outstanding' school leaders, *Educational Management and Administration,* 31(2)

Gold, R.L. (1958) Roles in sociological field observations, *Social Forces,* 36(3)

Goleman, D. (1998) *Working With Emotional Intelligence,* London: Bloomsbury

Gough, N. and Price, L. (2004) Rewording the World: Poststructuralism, deconstruction and the 'real' in environmental education, *South African Journal of Environmental Education,* (21)

Gray, J., Reynolds, D., Fitz-Gibbon, C. and Jesson, D. (1996) *Merging Traditions: The Future of Research on School Effectiveness and School Improvement,* London: Cassell

Gray, J., Hopkins, D., Reynolds, D., Wilcox, B., Farrell, S. and Jesson, D. (1999) *Improving Schools: Performance and Potential,* Buckingham: Open University Press

Greig, S., Pike, G. and Selby, D. (1989) *Greenprints For Changing Schools,* London: WWF and Kogan Page

Grima, D. (1996) 'Dinja Wahda' – a case study, in P. Pace (ed) *In Today's Education … Tomorrow's Environment,* Malta: mimeo

Gronn, P. (2000) Distributed properties: a new architecture for leadership, *Educational Management and Administration,* 28(3)

Gronn, P. (2002) Distributed leadership, in K. Leithwood, P. Hallinger, K. Seashore-Louis, G. Furman-Brown, P. Gronn, W. Mulford and K. Riley (eds) *The Second International Yearbook in Educational Leadership,* Dordrecht: Kluwer

Hadfield, M., Chapman, C., Curryer, I. and Barrett, P. (2002) *Building Capacity: Developing your School,* Nottingham: National College for School Leadership

198

Hargreaves, D. and Hopkins, D. (1991) *The Empowered School,* London, Cassell

Harris, A. (2002) *School Improvement – What's in it for Schools?* London: Routledge Falmer

Harris, A. and Chapman, C. (2002) *Effective Leadership in Schools Facing Challenging Circumstances,* Nottingham: National College for School Leadership

Hart, R. (1997) *Children's Participation: The Theory and Practice of Involving Young Citizens in Community Development and Environmental Care,* London: UNICEF/ Earthscan

Harvey, S. (2003) Looking to the future, *Ldr,* Nottingham: National College for School Leadership, 1(7)

Henderson, K. and Tilbury, D. (2004) *Whole School Approaches to Sustainability: An International Review of Sustainable School Programs,* Australian Research Institute in Education for Sustainability (ARIES) for the Department of the Environment and Heritage, Australian Government.

Hewton, E. (1988) *School Focussed Staff Development: Guidelines for Policy Makers,* Lewes: Falmer Press

Hicks, D. (2001) *Citizenship for the Future: A Practical Classroom Guide,* Godalming: WWF-UK

Hicks, D. and Holden, C. (1995) *Visions of the Future: Why We Need to Teach for Tomorrow,* Stoke on Trent: Trentham

(HMI) Her Majesty's Inspectorate of Education, (2001) *How good is our school?* Norwich: Her Majesty's Stationery Office

Hoban, G.F. and Erickson, G. (2004) Dimensions of learning for long-term professional development: comparing approaches from education, business and medical contexts, *Journal of In-Service Education,* 30(2)

Holden, C. (1998) Keen at 11, Cynical at 18? Encouraging Pupil Participation in School and Community, in C. Holden and N. Clough (eds) *op cit*

Holden, C. and Clough, N. (1998) The Child Carried on the Back does not Know the Length of the Road: The Teacher's Role in Assisting Participation, in C. Holden and N. Clough (eds) *op cit*

Holden, C. and Clough, N. (eds) (1998) *Children as Citizens: Education for Participation,* London: Jessica Kingsley

Hopkins, D. (ed) (1987) *Improving the Quality of Schooling,* London: Falmer Press

Hopkins, D. (2001) *School Improvement for Real,* London: Falmer Press

Hopkins, D., Ainscow, M. and West, M. (1994) School Improvement in an Era of Change, London: Cassell

Hopkins, D. and Harris, A. (1997) Understanding the school's capacity for development: growth states and strategies, *School Leadership and Management,* 17(3)

Howson, J. (2003) *The Relationship between Headteachers' Length of Service in Primary and Secondary Schools and Selected PANDA Grades,* Nottingham: National College for School Leadership.

Huckle, J. and Sterling, S. (1996) *Education for Sustainability,* London: WWF and Earthscan

(IUCN) International Union for the Conservation of Nature, (UNEP) United Nations Environment Programme and the (WWF) World Wide Fund for Nature (1991) *Caring for the Earth: A Strategy for Sustainable Living,* Gland, Switzerland: IUCN/UNEP/WWF

Jääskeläinen, L. and Nykänen, R. (1994) *Koulu ympäristön vaalijana,* Helsinki: Opetushallitus

James, A. and Prout, A. (eds) (1997) *Constructing and Reconstructing Childhood,* London: Falmer Press

Jensen, B.B. (2002) Knowledge Action and Pro-environmental Behaviour, *Environmental Education Research*, 8(3)

Jickling, B.J. (1992) Why I Don't Want my Children to be Educated for Sustainable Development, *Journal of Environmental Education*, 23(4)

John, M. (ed) (1996) *Children in Charge: One Child's Right to a Fair Hearing*, London: Jessica Kingsley

Joyce, B. and Showers, B. (1995) Learning experiences in staff development, *The Developer*, May 3

Kemmis, S. (1986) Action Research, in T. Husen and T. Postlethwaite (eds) *International Encyclopaedia of Education: Research and Studies, Volume I, A-B*. Oxford: Pergamon

Kimber, M. (2003) *Does Size Matter? Distributed leadership in a small secondary school, Practitioner Enquiry Report*, Nottingham: National College for School Leadership

Kohn, A. (2000) *The Case Against Standardized Testing: Raising the Scores, Ruining the Schools*, Portsmouth, NH: Heinemann

Kurttio, T. (1994) *Tuulinen polku: Muistiinpanoja ympäristökasvatuskokeilusta*, Helsinki: Painatuskeskus

Lambert, L. (1998) *Building Leadership Capacity in Schools*, Alexandria VA: ASCD

Lave, J. and Wenger, E. (1991) *Situated learning: Legitimate peripheral participation*, Cambridge: Cambridge University Press

Leal Filho, W. and Pace, P. (2002) Challenges to environmental education in the 21st century, in M. Alderweireldt (ed.) *Learning for a Sustainable Future: the Role of Communication, Ethics and Social Learning in Environmental Education*, Proceedings of the 8th Conference on Environmental Education in Europe, Gent: Belgium,10-14 September

Lewin, K. (1946) Action Research and Minority Problems, *Journal of Social Issues*, 26 (3)

Littledyke, M. (1997) Managerial style, the National Curriculum and teachers' culture: responses to educational change in a primary school, *Educational Research* 39 (3)

MacBeath, J. (ed) (1988) *Effective School Leadership: Responding to Change*, London: Paul Chapman

McCluney, R. (1994) Sustainable Values, in N.J. Brown and P. Quiblier (eds) *Ethics and Agenda 21: Moral Implications of a Global Consensus*, New York: United Nations Environment Programme

McLaughlin, R. (1991) Can the information systems for the NHS internal market work? *Public Money and Management*, Autumn

Ministry of Education (1986) *Law 46/86*, Lisbon: Diário da República

Ministry of Education (1991) *Law 1946/91*, Athens: Newspaper of the Greek Government

Ministry of Education (1994) *National Core Curriculum*, Helsinki: Opetushallitus

Ministry of Education (1999) *Creating the Future Together*, Malta: Ministry of Education

Ministry of Education and Science (2004) *Learning to change our world*, Stockholm: Ministry of Education and Science

Mogensen, F. (1995) School Initiatives related to Environmental Change – Development of Action Competence, in B.B. Jensen (ed) *Research in Environmental and Health Education*, Copenhagen: Royal Danish School of Educational Studies

Naess, A. (1995a) The Apron Diagram, in A. Drengson and Y. Inoue (eds) *The Deep Ecology Movement: An Introductory Anthology*, Berkley: North Atlantic Books

Naess, A. (1995b) The Place of Joy in a World of Fact and The Deep Ecology Movement: Some Philosophical Aspects, in G. Sessions (ed) *Deep Ecology for the 21st Century*, Boston: Shambhala Publications

National Commission of Education (1996) *Success Against the Odds*, London: Routledge

Nias, J., Southworth, G. and Yeomans, R. (1989) *Staff Relationships in the Primary School*, London: Cassell

Noutsos, X. (1983) *Aims of Education and Curriculum*, Athens: Dodoni

O'Sullivan, E. (1999) *Transformative learning: Educational vision for the 21st Century*, Toronto: University of Toronto Press and Zed Books

Oelschlaeger, M. (ed) (1995) *Postmodern Environmental Ethics*, Albany: State University of New York Press.

OECD (Organisation for Economic Cooperation and Development) (1993) *Take Pride in Pumpherston*, Dundee: Scottish Central Council on the Curriculum: SCCC

OECD (1994) *Environment, schools and active learning*, Final report of the environment and national schools' initiatives project (ENSI), Paris: OECD

OECD-CERI (Organisation for Economic Cooperation and Development – Centre for Educational Research and Innovation) (1995) *Environmental learning for the 21st century*, Paris: OECD

OECD/ENSI (Organisation for Economic Cooperation and Development/Environment and National Schools' Initiative) (1993) *Take Pride in Pumpherston*, Dundee: (SCCC) Scottish Consultative Council on the Curriculum

Orr, D.W. (1994) *Earth in Mind: On Education, Environment, and the Human Prospect*, Washington DC: Island Press

Orr, D.W (1996) Slow Knowledge, *Resurgence*, 196

Pace, P. (1992) The Environmental Education Programme – a Curriculum Development Project for the Primary School, Unpublished M.Ed. dissertation, Malta: Faculty of Education, University of Malta

Pace, P. (1996a) Top down planning in school-based environmental education, in C.M. Geesteranus (ed) *Planning Environmental Education: a Step or a Stride Forward*. Gland, Switzerland: International Union for the Conservation of Nature (IUCN)

Pace, P. (1996b) From Belgrade to Bradford – 20 years of environmental education, in W. Leal Filho, Z. Murphy, and K. O'Loan, (eds.) *A Sourcebook for Environmental Education*, London: Parthenon Publishing Group

Pace, P. (1997a) Environmental education in Malta: trends and challenges, *Environmental Education Research*, 3(1)

Pace, P. (1997b) Environmental Education and Teacher Education in Malta, Unpublished doctoral thesis, Bradford: University of Bradford

Pace, P. (2000) Attitudes towards environmental education in the Maltese formal education system, in W. Leal Filho (ed) *Communicating Sustainability, Environmental Education, Communication and Sustainability Series* (8), Frankfurt am Main: Peter Lang

Peterson B. (1999) La Escuela Fratney: a journey towards democracy, in M.W. Apple and J.A. Beane (eds) *op cit*

Pollard, A. (1985) *The Social World of the Primary School*, London: Cassell

Posch, P. (1993) Approaches to Values in Environmental Education, in OECD/ENSI *Values in Environmental Education Conference Report*, Dundee: Scottish Consultative Council on the Curriculum

Posch, P. (1996) Changing the Culture of Teaching and Learning: Implications for Action Research, in C. O'Hanlon (ed) *Professional Development through Action Research in Educational Settings*, London: Falmer Press

Posch, P. (1999) The Ecologisation of Schools and its Implications for Educational Policy, *Cambridge Journal of Education*, 29 (3)

Postman, N. and Weingartner, C. (1973) *Teaching As A Subversive Activity*, Harmondsworth: Penguin

Potter, D., Reynolds, D. and Chapman, C. (2002) School improvement for schools facing challenging circumstances: a review of research and practice, *School Leadership and Management*, 22(1)

Quarrie, J. (ed) (1992) *Earth Summit '92: The United Nations Conference on Environment and Development*, London: The Regency Press Corporation

Rauch, F. (2000) Schools: a place of ecological learning, *Environmental Education Research*, 6(3)

Reynolds, D. (1999) School effectiveness, school improvement and contemporary educational policies, in J. Demaine (ed) *Contemporary Educational Policy and Politics*, London: MacMillan

Rickinson, M. (2001) Learners and Learning in Environmental Education: a critical review of the research, *Environmental Education Research*, 7(3)

Ridley, M. (1996) *The Origins of Virtue*, London: Viking (Penguin)

Riley, K. and MacBeath, J. (1998) Effective leaders and effective schools, in J. MacBeath (ed.) *Effective School Leadership: Responding to Change*, London: Chapman

Robinson, J. (2003) Contemporary Globalization and Education, in S. Bartlett and D. Burton (eds) *Education Studies: Essential Issues*, London: Thousand Oaks and New Delhi: Sage

Robinson, J. and Shallcross, T. (1998) Social Change and Education for Sustainable Living, *Curriculum Studies*, 6 (1)

Robinson, V.M.J. (1993) *Problem-based Methodology: Research for the Improvement of Practice*, Oxford: Permagon

Roszak, T. (1995) Where Psyche Meets Gaia, in T. Roszak, M.E. Gomes and A.D. Kanner (eds) *Ecopsychology Restoring the Earth Healing the Mind*, San Francisco: Sierra Club Books

Rudduck, J. and Flutter, J. (2000) Pupil Participation and Pupil Perspective: 'carving a new order of experience,' *Cambridge Journal of Education*, 30(1)

Sachs, W. (1995) What Kind of Sustainability? *Resurgence*, 181

Sanger, J. with Willson, J. Davies, B. and Whittaker, R. (1997) *Young Children, Videos and Computer Games. Issues for Teachers and Parents*, London: Falmer Press

Sauvé, L. (1996) Environmental Education and Sustainable Development: further appraisal, *Canadian Journal of Environmental Education*, 1(1)

Sawatzki, M. (1997) Leading and managing staff for high performance, in B. Davies and L. Ellison (eds) *School Leadership for the 21st Century*, London: Routledge

Schall, E. (1995) Learning to love the swamp: reshaping education for public service, *Journal of Policy Analysis and Management*, 24(2)

Schnack, K. (1998) Why Focus on Conflicting Interests in Environmental Education? in M. Ahlberg and W. Leal Filho (eds) *Environmental Education for Sustainability: Good Environment, Good Life*, Frankfurt am Main: Peter Lang

Senge, P.M. (1990) *The Fifth Discipline*, New York: Doubleday

Sergiovanni, T. (2000) *The Lifeworld of Leadership*, London: Jossey-Bass

Shallcross, T. (2003) Education as Second Nature: Deep Ecology and School Development through Whole Institution Approaches to Sustainability Education, Unpublished PhD thesis, Manchester: Manchester Metropolitan University

Shallcross, T. (ed) (2004) *School Development Through Whole School Approaches to Sustainability Education: The SEEPS Project*, Manchester: Manchester Metropolitan University

Shallcross, T., O'Loan, K. and Hui, D. (2000) Developing A School-focused Approach to Continuing Professional Development in Sustainability Education, *Environmental Education Research*, 6(4)

Shiva, V. (1992) Recovering the real meaning of sustainability, in D.E. Cooper and J. Palmer (eds) *The Environment in Question Ethics and Global Issues*, Routledge: London

Shulman, L.S. (1987) Knowledge and Teaching: Foundations of the New Reform, *Harvard Educational Review*, 57(1)

Smyth, J. and Hattam, R. (2002) Early School Leaving and the Cultural Geography of High Schools, *British Educational Research Journal*, 28(3)

Stables, A. (2001) Language and Meaning in Environmental Education: an overview, *Environmental Education Research*, 7(2)

Stanley, L. (2004) A Methodological Toolkit for Feminist Research: Analytical Reflexivity, Accountable Knowledge, Moral Epistemology and Being 'A Child of Our Time,' in H. Piper and I. Stronach (eds) *Educational Research: Difference and Diversity*, Aldershot: Ashgate Publishing

Stapp, W.B., Wals, A.E.J. and Stankorb, S. (1996) *Environmental education for empowerment: action research and community problem solving*, Dubuque, Iowa: Kendall/Hunt Publishers

Sterling, S. (2001) *Sustainable Education: Revisioning Learning and Change*, Dartington: Green Books

Stokes, E., Edge, A. and West, A. (2001) *Environmental education in the educational systems of the European Union*, Brussels: Environment Directorate-General of the European Commission

Stoll, L. and Fink, D. (1996) *Changing our Schools: Linking School Effectiveness and School Improvement*, Buckingham: Open University Press

Stringfield, S. (1995) Attempting to enhance students' learning through innovative programs: the case for schools evolving into high reliability organisations, *School Effectiveness and School Improvement*, 6(1)

Surgrue, C. (2002) Irish teachers' experiences of professional learning: implications for policy and practice, *Journal of In-Service Education*, 28(2)

Tamoutseli, K. (1999) *Outdoors School Setting: An Educational Tool*, Thessaloniki: EEC Makrynitsa

Tanti, V.M. (2000) Environmental Education in Maltese Government Schools: Historical Review, Unpublished B.Ed. (Hons) dissertation, Malta: Faculty of Education, University of Malta

Tasker, M. (2001) Penalties of Scale, *Resurgence*, 207

Teddlie, C. and Reynolds, D. (2000) *The International Handbook of School Effectiveness Research*, London: Falmer

Tooley, J. (2000) *Reclaiming Education*, London: Cassell

United Nations (1989) *Convention on the Rights of the Child*, http://www.unicef.org/crc/crc.htm

United Nations (UN) (2000) *Millennium Development Goals*, www.un.org/millennium goals/

UNESCO (1978) *Intergovernmental Conference on Environmental Education*, Tbilisi: UNESCO

UNESCO (1997) *Educating for a Sustainable Future: A Transdisciplinary Vision for Concerted Action*, Paris: UNESCO

UNESCO (2004) *United Nations Decade of Education for Sustainable Development 2005-2014: Draft International Implementation Scheme*, Paris: UNESCO

UNESCO-UNEP (1988) *International Strategy for Action in the Field of Environmental Education and Training for the 1990s*, Paris/Nairobi: UNESCO – UNEP

University of Turku (1997) *Our Common Environment: Soil, Water and Air*, Turku: University of Turku

Uzzell, D., Davallon, J., Fontes, P. J., Gottesdiener, H., Jensen, B.B., Kofoed, J., Uhrenholdt, G. and Vognsen, C. (1994) *Pupils as Catalysts of Environmental Change*, Brussels: European Commission Directorate General for Science Research and Development

Uzzell, D. (1999) Education for Environmental Action in the Community: new roles and relationships, *Cambridge Journal of Education*, 29(33).

van Matre, S. (1990) *Earth education... a new beginning*, Cedar Cove, West Virginia: Institute of Earth Education

Vognsen, C. (1995) The QUARK programme, a Collaboration on the Development of Environmental Education and Ecological Technologies in Local Communities, in B. B. Jensen (ed) *Research in Environmental and Health Education*, Copenhagen, Royal Danish School of Educational Studies

Walker, K., Corcoran, P.B. and Wals, A.E.J. (2004) Case Studies, Make-Your-Case Studies, and Case Stories: A Critique of Case Study Methodology in Sustainability in Higher Education, *Environmental Education Research*, 10(1)

Wals, A.E.J. (1993) Critical phenomenology and environmental education research, in R. Mrazek (ed) *Alternative Paradigms in Environmental Education Research*, Ohio/USA: North American Association of Environmental Education

Wals, A.E.J., Beringer, A. and Stapp, W.B. (1990) Education in action: a community problem-solving program for schools, *The Journal of Environmental Education*, 21(4)

Wals, A.E.J. and Alblas, A.H. (1997) School-based research and development of environmental education: a case study. *Environmental Education Research*, 3(3)

Wals, A.E.J. and Jickling, B. (2002) 'Sustainability' in higher education: from doublespeak and newspeak to critical thinking and meaningful learning, *Higher Education Policy*, 15

WCED, (The World Commission on Environment and Development) (1987) *Our Common Future*, Oxford: Oxford University Press

Wenger, E. (1999) *Communities of Practice: Learning, Meaning and Identity*, Cambridge: Cambridge University Press

West, M., Hopkins, D. and Beresford, J. (1995) Conditions for school and classroom development, paper presented at the *European Conference on Educational Research*, University of Bath, 14th -17th September

Wilson, E.O. (2002) *The Future of Life*, London: Little, Brown Books

Woods, P. (1996) *Researching the Art of Teaching: ethnography for educational use*, London: Routledge

(WWF) Worldwide Fund for Nature (2005) *Linking Thinking: New perspectives on thinking and learning for sustainability*, Aberfeldy: WWF Scotland

York-Barr, J., Sommers, W., Ghere, G. and Montie, J. (2001) *Reflective Practice to Improve Schools: an Action Guide for Educators*, California: Corwin Press Inc

Zimmerman, M. E. (1988) Quantum Theory, Intrinsic Value and Panentheism, in M. Oelschlaeger (ed) *Postmodern Environmental Ethics*, New York: State University of New York Press

Index